THE LEADER WHO CARES

Guiding Human Resource Practitioners to Navigate Workplace Environments

Nikki Pounds, MHRD, SPHR, SHRM-CP

SPARK Publications
Charlotte, North Carolina

The Leader Who CARES
Guiding Human Resources Practitioners to
Navigate Workplace Environments

Nikki Pounds

Illustrations
Kraphix / shutterstock.com
Illustrations by SPARK Publications

Designed, produced, and published by SPARK Publications
SPARKpublications.com
Charlotte, North Carolina

Printed in the United States of America

Paperback, May 2023, ISBN: 978-1-953555-46-5
Hardback, May 2023, ISBN: 978-1-953555-49-6
Ebook, May 2023, ISBN: 978-1-953555-50-2

Library of Congress Control Number: 2023905606

DEDICATION

I dedicate my first book to my husband and daughters, Greg, Jordan, and Sydney, who encouraged me, believed in me, and supported me throughout this very long journey. I am blessed beyond measure because I get to coexist with you!

To the entire SPARK Publications team—your coaching and expertise were invaluable. I appreciate all of you for the guidance that allowed me to make this happen.

Contents

Content warning: this book contains references to rape and sexual assault.

ACKNOWLEDGMENTS

To all the wonderful leaders I have the pleasure of knowing personally, and those I have admired from afar, I would like to thank you for inspiring me to inspire others.

My heartfelt thanks go out to Herman Moore, Jason Wolf, John Ezzo, John Costello, and Dr. Lisa Wicker for contributing your leadership expertise and unwavering support. I am forever grateful to have each of you in my life as mentors and friends.

INTRODUCTION

There is a difference between a boss and a leader. An individual can be in a leadership position but not respect people, the organization, or sometimes even themselves. A true leader has a vision which they articulate in ways that inspire, motivate, and engage the people around them. When I am describing a true leader, they will be referred to as such.

I have had bosses who thought they were leaders, but in reality, they were not. These so-called leaders bossed their employees around, and because they were in positions of authority, they thought that by bossing employees around and telling people what to do, it made them a leader. I don't prefer the term "boss," but I use it throughout the book to make a point.

There are articles, white papers, and maybe even a book or two that bore us with the theoretical reasons some bosses are not good leaders and why others are outstanding leaders. The following is not your typical leadership self-help book. The narrative may offend some bosses that are really bullies. So, if that is true of you, I would caution you to read further only if your mirror is clean enough to see your reflection in it.

This book is about ownership, accountability, and the raw, unadulterated truth about situations that I may, or may not, have encountered throughout my many years in corporate Human Resources (HR). When I began my journey, it was known as Personnel, and I had no idea I would make it a career. I most certainly did not know that twenty-seven years later I would write a book chronicling my experiences and sharing the experiences of others.

I have grown to love many aspects about this profession; however, there are facets that I hate. As you read further, my hope is that you will understand the love-hate relationship I have with HR and why, over many years, it has become my passion.

My Path to a Career in Human Resources

At the ripe old age of seventeen, I interviewed for a cooperative (co-op) education position and was afforded the opportunity to work for a manufacturing company in the small town of Chester, South Carolina, where I was born and raised. Several companies partnered with our one local high school to hire students to help with projects that they did not have time to complete. These opportunities also helped students gain vital experience that would aid in their growth as adults and professionals.

Co-op roles, internships, and apprenticship programs were a dying breed for some time and have now been revitalized as older generations brace themselves for a crop of young folks eager to take over. These work experiences the companies provided—and are now providing again—are more of what business owners and leaders would consider win-win scenarios. I would love to see more of these opportunities offered to high school and college students in this day and time, so they can get a taste of the real world and start making real-life decisions instead of theoretical ones.

Back to the co-op. These companies employed cheap high school labor to clean basements, file paperwork, and undertake other work that was otherwise despised by the regular full-time staff members. Lucky for me, I lived in a small town. A very close family member that was professionally acquainted with the personnel manager of the manufacturing company put in a call and spoke highly of me. I know what you are thinking, so I will say it for you: I am 100 percent sure the call she made put me ahead of the other students that interviewed for the role. Some might say that it was not *what* I knew, but *who* I knew that landed me in this pivotal role. They might be right. However, after receiving the opportunity and while I was in the role, I showed up on time every day. I performed the tasks that had been assigned to me and I challenged myself with learning everything I could about the job. I wanted to contribute as much as I could to the organization, although I had very little knowledge about what I was really doing. Nevertheless, I landed the role and performed amazingly well.

My primary tasks included filing new personnel records and paperwork in the file cabinets, which were located in the main office. Additionally, I was tasked with (and this was probably the main reason they created the job) purging old personnel files in the dark, dingy, cold, spider- and rodent-infested basement. I told no one exactly what I was doing because I was a little embarrassed by the minutiae of it all. I understood that just like in the movie *The Karate Kid*, I was the Daniel to Mr. Miyagi. If you don't know who I'm talking about, google it.

The personnel manager was an extremely kind gentleman, so he did not insist that I spend all my days in the basement. When we had the occasion to speak, he would speak to me as he would any of his other team members, and I respected him for that. Besides being a great example of a leader, being empathetic and fair, he also taught me two other very valuable lessons: how to process payroll and that people are nebulous. These two things may seem trivial, but they absolutely are not. They are critical components of HR but on opposite ends of the spectrum. Payroll is highly tactical, and dealing with ambiguity is highly strategic.

"The most significant point to remember when you are processing payroll," as he stated, "is to always look at payroll as just numbers." I was to never look at each employee's salary and think that I should earn what they are earning. He rightfully stressed such things as that these are just numbers and that my job when calculating and checking those numbers is to ensure they match and the totals are accurate; nothing more, nothing less. No employee is here on a volunteer basis, so pay attention and get it right the first time.

In order to be successful, I had to deal with ambiguity and function in the gray. Although policies or procedures were written quite specifically, situations that arose had to be handled differently based on each employee's circumstances. I learned that fair is not always equal. These two very important lessons have been embedded in my psyche ever since and have helped me remain objective in my decision-making and handling of people in the workplace.

At that time, the most important jobs of the personnel department were to pay employees, hire the right people, fire the wrong people, and treat people fairly. I appreciate those lessons today because for many years I could overlook the fact that many team members earned more money than me. I never complained about salary—well, maybe once, but that story is for another book. And I treated similarly situated employees equally, which meant that I was being fair. In HR, we use the phrase "similarly situated" to describe employees who are in the same or similar role in the company, or those who are in completely different roles but are paid using the same or a similar formula. I did and still do function in the gray and ensure people are paid properly.

The co-op role in the personnel department of the local manufacturing company in my small hometown propelled me to obtain an internship in the recruiting department at Spartanburg Regional Healthcare System in Spartanburg, South Carolina, the city where I attended college. This time, no one made a phone call on my behalf. I interviewed for the internship along with sixteen other students from various universities, and I landed the job all on my own.

The news, current world affairs, random facts, and learning as much about everything as I could have always captivated me. I still get goose bumps when I recall the one fact I knew that impressed the leaders of the hospital so much that it made me stand out from the pack. Getting noticed at work and positioning oneself to be unforgettable is a technique, but as a hopeful intern, I was just being me.

The random fact that I recalled during the interview was that on January 1, 1993, Czechoslovakia dissolved, and the split created the Czech Republic and Slovakia. I knew the background of what is sometimes known as the "Velvet Divorce." Understanding the reason for the division, I could speak in great length about it with the hospital management staff and recruiters. I knew what I wanted, and fortunately, this random fact was part of the reason that I landed the internship. That internship was another integral part of my growth in HR.

I completed my internship with the hospital in the summer of 1994 and graduated in May 1996 from the University of South Carolina Spartanburg, now called the University of South Carolina Upstate, to be more inclusive of the entire South Carolina upstate region. Shortly after graduation and while I was working full time as a teller at a local bank (I cannot for the life of me remember the name), a position became available in the recruiting department at the hospital in which I interned. I had never recruited and did not intern in recruiting, but I knew the recruiting department was an extension of the HR department, so I applied. They contacted me to schedule an interview. I interviewed, completed a series of assessments, and once again landed the role all on my own.

During my time with the hospital system, I mostly had contact with hospital managers and staff, not so much with doctors and other practitioners. Although my role was to onboard locum tenens once they were hired and settled in their temporary, fully furnished apartments, I did not interact with them much afterwards. Locum tenens is Latin for "a worker who temporarily takes the place of another with similar qualifications, for example as a doctor or a member of the clergy."[1] In laypeople's terms, I assisted with hiring traveling physicians and mostly onboarded them and took care of the details of their assignments within the hospital. The physicians were hired to work with the hospital or an affiliated practice of the hospital system for twelve to eighteen months and then they were off to work at the next hospital. I spoke with the physicians over the phone and some in person when they were available. I don't even know if platforms like WebEx, Zoom, or Skype were available at that time, but I know we didn't use them. The process consisted of an in-depth, over-the-phone interview. The hospital needed physicians and was constantly hiring; therefore, the process of interviews, relocation, and onboarding was a full-time position and fairly new to the hospital system at that time. Once a physician was hired, I provided instructions for their temporary housing, allowances, per diems, and other pertinent details of their contract.

During my time there, I reentered school to get my master's degree. I was working with hospital managers who all had master-level degrees or above, and I thought I would surely remain there for the long haul. So, being the ambitious type of person, I applied and was admitted into Clemson University, where I entered their newly created Master of Human Resources Development program.

By the time I was twenty-five years old, I was married, had obtained a bachelor's degree in psychology and a master's degree in human resources development, and had four years of HR experience under my belt. During this time, I encountered many leaders who were ethical, honorable, and authentic. I also had the displeasure of working with bully bosses who were unethical, selfish, and reckless. Their actions and inactions are forever etched in my mind; hence the reason I wrote a book about leadership and culture.

Encountering paradoxical people who had risen to leadership levels afforded me many opportunities to provide advice about handling situations that my closest friends and family faced regularly. Whenever I attended an event or engaged in casual conversations and people would inquire about my HR profession, they would ask my opinion about dealing with a complicated situation that involved a manager, peer, or even a subordinate. When speaking with friends or family members who were starting their own business, they would reach out to me for advice about employee handbooks, the best way to handle an employee who was behaving badly, unemployment claims, or ask me to take part in the interview process for a position they were hiring for within their growing organization. I happily used my intuition and pragmatic approach to advise others.

In providing advisement as well as receiving advice from mentors, coaches, and counsel when handling legal situations, I retained a considerable amount of knowledge about how leadership, or the lack thereof, can cause a tremendous strain on the consciousness of people and the reputation of organizations. My Human Resources and Leadership Development firm, HR Unequivocally®, was born out of the need to provide a pragmatic approach to businesses and organizational leaders who want to understand what is going wrong with their employee engagement, innovation, and their lack of ability to keep the most talented human capital available. "Unequivocal" is defined as leaving no doubt, being clear or unambiguous. Therefore, I created the CARES Leadership Model® as a tool that other HR practitioners can use to evaluate **C**ulture, **A**uthenticity, **R**espect, **E**motional **I**ntelligence, and **S**upport.

Unfortunately, I have witnessed some of the worst cases of poor leadership imaginable. Some of those bosses were deceptive and others may have meant well, but they simply did not embody the leadership characteristics needed to create a healthy culture to ensure employees delivered exceptional organizational results. Their actions are less of an aberration than a reflection of what unchecked behavior can yield in terms of creating and maintaining toxic workplace cultures. Some of those bosses did not understand the techniques that are necessary in handling difficult situations appropriately. The mishandling of destructive behaviors led to exemplary employees becoming complacent and delivering mediocre results at best.

This book will discuss each of the five laws of CARES in sections. In the first chapter of each section, I will give you examples of a poor bully boss. The following chapter will discuss great examples of leadership. Last, I will discuss each of the five leadership laws in detail and provide organizational questions for reflection. It is my hope that this book will assist you, my fellow HR practitioner, in helping our leaders focus on the qualities that make a good leader so we can serve as role models to help propel the organization's culture.

culture

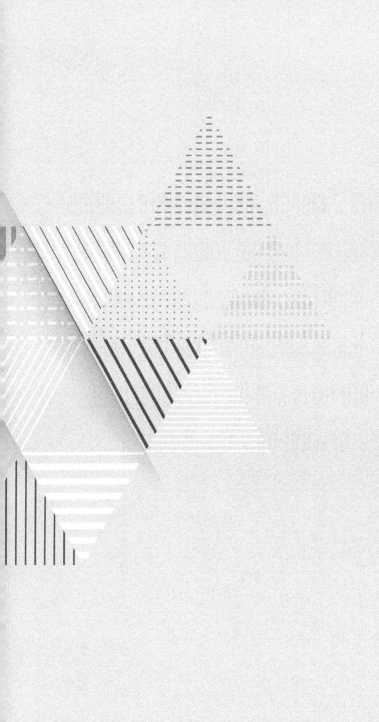

"Great company cultures are created when we live the values we say are important. Values diminish when leaders create subcultures that are toxic and the direct opposite of what they say is valued."

CHAPTER 1

The Day the Walls Shook

Anyone who knows me knows I love a wonderfully delicious meal and will spend megabucks on great food. I know we should eat to live, but I feel like in many instances I live to eat. Often, I am already planning what dinner will consist of when we haven't even finished lunch. You might say that my life revolves around food.

When it is time to eat, it is time to eat. Great conversation and a glass of wine before a meal are the perfect complement to creating an exceptional dining experience. However, whether the meal arrives at my table in a restaurant, at a friend's or family member's table in their home, or if I have prepared a meal, when the food is done and plated, bon appétit.

You are probably thinking, Who cares about how much you love to eat? What's the point, lady? Let me explain. I want you to feel the passion I have in my heart and soul for food. If you can appreciate my love for food or, better yet, relate to it, you will understand why I think the bully boss I describe in this chapter was so disrespectful. There are many reasons I consider them disrespectful, which I will also explain, but the most important scenarios have something, at least a little, to do with food.

To Eat, or Not to Eat? That Is the Question

There was a fantastic restaurant that served authentic Italian food, and luckily it was within walking distance of our office. Occasionally for lunch, we would order from that little Italian restaurant because not only did they consistently serve delicious meals, the service was impeccable. The aroma of Italy filled the office as soon as the first dish arrived.

Various types of pasta made daily with homemade marinara, eggplant parmesan, antipasto salad, minestrone, and the world's best lasagna were handcrafted with love and delivered right to our door. Tiramisu and cannoli, of course, all made from scratch daily, were staples and just one part of the meal that we so looked forward to each time. If your mouth is not watering yet, it should be!

The team was drawn to the conference room where the self-serve dishes were neatly aligned in a row, nestled in their respective chafing dishes, and where plates, cutlery, and crisp white linen napkins awaited us. The company and leaders appreciated a sumptuous meal too and respected us enough to order lunch so that we used our time wisely by eating lunch while holding a meeting. This sounds reasonable, right? Wrong!

The CEO enters the room thirty minutes after we had partaken of the delicious meal. In fact, half of the team were making their way back for seconds. The other half were standing over the desserts, contemplating and trying to make one of the hardest decisions they would make that day: Should I have an entire piece of tiramisu and a cannoli? Or should I have half of the tiramisu and half of a cannoli?

Back to the CEO—they enter the room with a sour face. Everyone else in the room was all smiles because we had eaten some great food and were ready with our documents, charts, facts, data, and discussion points to engage in another productive meeting. We were puzzled because we had such delicious food and all invitees to the meeting were present, yet the CEO did not seem pleased. They stormed out of the room and slammed the door. The walls shook! Artwork dropped to the floor from the vibration, papers blew off tables, and notebooks rattled from the door being slammed so hard. We all shuddered, to say the least. Then we asked ourselves and eventually each other, "What just happened?"

After some time of sitting, thinking, and replaying what happened, the administrative assistant sheepishly revealed that the CEO was upset because we ate before they arrived. When they entered the room, plates were empty, and some were pondering which desserts to have, all while laughing and enjoying the moment. They quietly told their assistant that we were disrespectful because we didn't wait for them. They thought we should never have dined before they arrived.

When the leader of an organization orders food for a lunch meeting and is late, on purpose or by chance, they should not expect their employees to wait for them before eating. Respecting your team members enough to be on time for a meeting that you initiated is the least one could ask for. Respecting people enough to not expect them to wait thirty minutes for you to arrive because you want to dictate should never be burdensome. Unfortunately, it was quite a burden for this bully boss. Although respect was a core value for this particular organization, the subculture of disrespect was created and ran deep throughout it. I often say, "Great company cultures are created when we live the values we say are important. Values diminish when leaders create subcultures that are toxic and the direct opposite of what they say is valued."

R-E-S-P-E-C-T

Respect is relative and means different things to different people. Respect is difficult to measure but easy to see. Even back in 1967, Otis Redding wrote a famous song for the illustrious Aretha Franklin, expounding the virtues of respect. We all want it. All of us need it. We desire respect not only in our personal life, but it should be an important part of a company's culture.

The actions of the CEO on the day the walls shook came about because we refused to continue being disrespected. You see, this was not the first time we were on the receiving end of their disrespectful behavior. We didn't plan to eat before the CEO arrived. We didn't discuss it or conspire to piss them off. We were fed up, and that day was the day that we pushed back. The reality was, we knew something would happen. We just didn't know what. Measuring respect is nearly impossible, but in this case, did we need to assign a number to the level of disrespect we received to know that it existed?

In a culturally healthy company, people feel respected and know their opinions matter. Relationships are strong and people feel a sense of loyalty for the company as engagement increases. They feel empowered to eat at the scheduled start time of a meeting!

"Culture is the standard
bearer of performance."

—Jason Wolf

CHAPTER 2

Develop a Culture of Gratitude

I had the pleasure of speaking with Jason Wolf, cofounder of Wolf Garretson and owner of The Brooklyn Collective, located in the historic Brooklyn neighborhood in Charlotte, North Carolina. Jason is an ally for communities of marginalized people and is the epitome of servant leadership.

The Brooklyn community was home to restaurants, theaters, insurance firms, printing companies and other thriving businesses, a mix of upscale and low-income housing, churches, a YMCA, schools, and a library that was built by Black people for Black people. In the past, in Charlotte and surrounding areas, Blacks were not served in many restaurants, could not purchase homes in certain neighborhoods, and were not welcomed at other YMCAs and libraries, so they built their own.[2] Black professionals financed the Mecklenburg Investment Company Building (MIC) to provide an office space for Black residents and neighbors. This building still remains.

Approval from the federal government allowed Charlotte's Redevelopment Commission to tear down homes they considered substandard for living, and from 1960 to 1967, 1,480 homes were torn down, displacing 1,007 families, and most of 200 plus businesses were demolished. Promises were made to those business owners and families that their neighborhood would be restored.[3] To date, that has not happened.

Jason researched the history of the property he purchased and realized that it held such fond historic memories to many, and much anger from some—particularly the former residents. The former residents' families and the many activists are still fighting for answers and justice. Jason knew immediately that he wanted the buildings he purchased to serve a similar purpose today. Besides becoming one of Charlotte's most popular places for well-known and new artists, The Brooklyn Collective is now home to businesses owned by people of color, including mine. There is so much more to know about the Brooklyn community, now known as The Brooklyn Collective. I encourage you to visit the website to access resources and read about the collective's history at https://www.brooklyncollectiveclt.org.

"Gratitude at Work"

Now, let's get into the reason Jason is an example of an outstanding leader: culture. Jason says a company's culture creates a baseline for accepted behavior. Through his time cofounding and building Garretson Resolution Group (GRG), a claims administration firm that administered payments to claimants for high-profile settlements, such as the National Football League's concussion settlement, the Deepwater Horizon's oil spill, and the first responders settlement from the World Trade Center attacks after the horrendous events that took place on September 11, 2001, Jason and his business partner have as much respect for Human Resources (HR) as they do for any other function within an organization.

Some leaders think of HR as a necessary evil. Jason does not. Jason and his business partner had a lot of false starts when it came to HR, and they learned the hard way how important it is to have HR in a "seat at the table" as an independent voice to make strategic decisions. He understands that employing the function of HR is a luxury for a small business, but one that he realizes is necessary for helping drive a culture of community servitude, respect, hard work, and hard play. He described the GRG culture as one of "Gratitude at Work."

Gratitude was Jason and his partner's standard for communicating with clients and claimants. Training was certainly a part of building a culture of gratitude, but being a role model and living the values as owners of the business also affected how employees behaved. All the staff knew what was expected of them. Much of the social impact of the company's culture of gratitude grew into charitable events that engaged the workforce so they could be involved in the decisioning of where quarterly monetary distributions would be allocated and how they could spend their time volunteering. Although there was a financial component to their culture of gratitude, team members could also spend time physically supporting organizations that needed people's time and talents. Jason and his business partner needed real servant leaders, not theoretical ones. Gratitude extended beyond the four walls of GRG, and they made and continued to make a significant impact on the communities in which the company serves. They lived their values every single day.

Internally, though, Jason described how programs of gratitude evolved out of the ideas from employees and grew organically. Whether it was organizing social functions, refining the performance review process, or seeking candidates at job fairs, all of it was executed while maintaining a culture of gratitude, which was at the forefront of all activities. Jason stated, "When employees see the founders living the culture and the employees have a voice and ownership at work, adoption is much different than when people feel like an initiative was just announced without input or consideration for them."

As a business owner and leader in his organization, initially it surprised Jason just how much people looked to him to set the culture. When employees watched him lead calls with clients, that set the tone of not only gratitude but being client-centric. I asked Jason how their team members, capital, and technology grew without losing their culture of gratitude. He made a very important point in that he and his business partner had to be strong enough to bring in other strong people with the right attributes, and those people became the gatekeepers of the culture. They became ambassadors. One of his favorite sayings is "iron sharpens iron," so surround yourself with great people, who are sharp, and great things will happen in your company.

Jason says, "Culture is the standard bearer of performance." Performance is all about the way a culture is defined and lived, meaning it is how clients and claimants are respected throughout the process, what responses they receive, and how timely the responses are.

Culture is multifaceted and has a lot to do with people's moral compass. From the onset, GRG established "Gratitude at Work" and walked the talk, which allowed employees to be involved in their community and maintain that culture at work, without many misaligned subcultures popping up here and there.

Jason's company, GRG, lived its cultural values and made a significant positive impact on their employees and society, as evidenced by how they treat each other now and how they continue to give back to the communities they serve. If, as a leader in your organization, HR business partner, or otherwise, you are saying you live certain values and you do not display those values by your behavior, you will lose the confidence of your workforce and they unequivocally will not be engaged. We must present the value of what we do to our leaders and show them how HR contributes to the success of the company.

This is especially true if we were to encounter the Jason Wolf of eighteen years ago, who was uninformed and unaware of the impact a strategic HR partner could make on their business. In Jason's first role out of college, leaders told team members that if they did a good job, their weekly contract would be renewed. That was the culture in the company he worked for back then, and judging by that one comment I would dare say the culture must have been quite scary. This mindset resonates with me because I have experienced bosses who think of HR and their team members this way.

One of the best lessons Jason learned about partnering with a knowledgeable HR professional was that, although he could find someone to do the job, without strategic thought, Jason's culture would suffer. He compared it to taxes. He could find a tax preparer to do the job, but he would not receive the strategic thought that a Certified Public Accountant could bring. It was no different with HR. Jason thought he could handle people and culture all by himself until he found they were stumbling around talent management. He then realized that having a strategic HR voice was important for the growth of the company.

As Jason puts it, "HR is more than trust fall exercises!" He believes that every employee in a business is critical to the growth of the company because that person's actions will determine and influence whether clients are happy with the quality of service that is provided. A strategic voice to help cultivate best practices around culture and talent management leads to happy employees. And happy employees ensure their clients are happy. This alone can be the difference between a successful company and an unsuccessful one.

Now, turn your attention to the associated solutions and alternatives that involve the HR function using a strategic approach that will either restrict or accelerate the growth of an organization. This approach will have a lasting impact on every stakeholder.

CHAPTER 3

Leadership Law #1: Culture

Your Human Resources (HR) department may or may not have the power to change the culture immediately, but with time, HR professionals can undoubtedly influence senior leaders to move the culture in a positive direction.

To impact company culture, create ways to evaluate it and make a strategic plan to maximize the culture's impact on the bottom line. While you are calculating turnover, collecting data, and creating strategic plans, remember that your voice must be heard. As an HR professional, you must stand for what you know is right for the people as well as the company.

At its core, culture equals the values and traditions that founders of the organization, or those who are now responsible for it, find most important. Every person has a unique personality. Each individual has their preferences, experiences, and beliefs, and so does every organization. Organizational cultures may be similar, but there are always nuances that make one organization different from the next, just as it is with people.

Culture is created before the first employee is hired and is largely influenced by what the owners and leaders spend time on. When a company grows to the level of being beyond what the owner can handle, cultures tend to shift and take on traits new leaders bring with them. When this happens, the cultural shift could be positive or negative.

To survive, businesses must remain flexible and respond to consumer needs, which are ever changing. Marketing, business development, key resources, streams of income, products, and services are aspects of businesses that are evaluated continuously to remain competitive. Unfortunately, culture is often a fleeting thought in the minds of business owners and leaders until the organization finds itself on the wrong side of a lawsuit. Culture isn't considered important until valuable employees depart in droves, or at the very least, employees complain until they are heard. Until HR professionals tie cultural impact to bottom-line numbers and get the attention of the cultural elite, it will not get the consideration it deserves.

When the culture influencers realize that turnover costs employers an average of 33 percent of an employee's annual salary to replace them, as reported by Employee Benefit News,[4] they may perk up. I would argue that turnover costs are much more than 33 percent, but we'll stick with this number for now. Tracking turnover closely is one way to present data to get your executives' attention and help them realize that culture matters. If you are not tracking turnover and assigning a dollar amount to it based on salary data and replacement costs, you are doing your department and your organization a disservice. Know your numbers. Know your turnover percentages and the replacement cost for each role to articulate the true bottom-line effect. As I stated earlier, many areas of the business are under a microscope continuously, but for some reason, culture is assessed once every few years through an employee engagement survey or focus group sessions.

Assessing your culture is critical to improve talent attraction and engagement. Culture drives performance. When you allow a toxic culture to maintain the status quo or when you don't know what is important to people, you cannot effectively define performance standards. We talk a lot about retention, but what is most important is engagement. When leaders create toxic cultures and HR professionals have limited power or capacity to change it, exemplary employees will become disengaged and will eventually leave the organization, which can lead to low employee morale and even more toxicity.

It is important to build a structural foundation to consistently evaluate our organization's culture. Culture continues to be a major factor in an organization's ability to attract, engage, and retain employees. In addition to presenting relevant data related to culture, we can answer the following questions for our leaders.

Organizational Reflection Questions

1	How does my organization's culture impact policies, practices, and procedures?
2	Do my organization's policies, practices, and procedures positively guide the behavior we expect our leaders and employees to exhibit? How? How not?
3	How can I, as an HR professional, influence organizational culture?
4	What gaps have I identified in our organization that could be addressed to support a positive culture?
5	What is the most effective way to propose filling these gaps to senior leaders in order to have an impact on creating a positive culture?

6	Can we clearly articulate our organizational culture?
7	Are we consistent in articulating the culture?
8	Do we believe what we say about our culture? If so, what specific examples can I provide to exhibit that we live our culture? If not, what behaviors are not aligned with what we say our culture is?
9.	Has our culture helped or hindered our recruiting efforts?
10.	How has our culture improved workforce engagement? Be specific.
11.	How has our culture decreased workforce engagement and morale? Be specific.

authenticity

"Authentic leaders are strong enough to be vulnerable and wise enough to know that vulnerability does not make them weak."

CHAPTER 4

"The Great Influencer" . . . Not!

You cannot fake authenticity, no matter how much you try! Sure, for a little while, anyone can send their representative out to play, but eventually the real person will show up most likely sooner rather than later. They always do. Challenge their opinion, know more than they do in one area or another, or have a stronger relationship with the person they would like to align themselves with and boy oh boy, the real person will undoubtedly rear their ugly head. On the other side of the invisible continuum, there are many authentic leaders who don't have an ugly head to rear, and you will also know that sooner rather than later.

Keeping the Score

One bully boss in particular would build trust with employees by asking about their families and even going so far as to remember their family members' names, all the while pretending to care. The ability to remember specifics about family members and their situations is such a special quality to have as a leader, and he certainly had a gift for remembering a great deal of relevant details. When an employee's child was sick or they requested some sort of short- or long-term leave to care for a parent or spouse, he would remember their circumstances and inquire about it later to ensure all was well and being handled at home.

Early on, we thought he cared about us and our family's well-being. Little did we know our personal lives would be used against us later. Many of us were confronted with the cold, hard truth when we needed time off or requested to work remotely. He was counting the times an employee needed a concession to handle a situation outside of work. In essence, he kept the score!

Knowing specific details about instances that affected employees and the accommodations that were made so that employees could take care of their personal affairs was not the problem. The concern was that he used those rare occasions of taking time away from the office to chastise employees in front of their colleagues at the most unexpected times. Employees complained about it occasionally and we believed them, but it was difficult to imagine how such a conversation would occur because his concern seemed so genuine—at first. I truly wanted to trust that he thought his behavior was acceptable because, as we all know from Management 101, you praise in public and reprimand in private.

On the surface, the leader of an organization showing concern for what we would consider as insignificant for such a high-ranking leader gives cause for concern, but when leaders follow the CARES Leadership Model®, are self-aware and transparent, lead by example, and possess all the other qualities of great leaders, it's not so bad. Unfortunately, those impressive leadership qualities did not exist within this bully boss. His lack of authenticity permeated throughout the organization and ultimately created a toxic culture of distrust and disrespect, which led to the demise of several great working relationships with employees who had once produced stellar work and were fully engaged.

I realize now that he did not know how to be authentic. You may think to yourself that it's easier to be authentic than to try to be someone else all the time. Generally, that is the case. But unfortunately, this bully boss learned his insidious ways from other bully bosses he thought were leaders. No one had ever told him differently or confronted his behavior in a bold way. He had been judged and ridiculed in front of peers in previous roles. Although he knew it didn't create a sense of security and psychological safety for him, he emulated that behavior to get the promotions and power he longed for. His company promoted that type of behavior. Although one of the core values of the company was caring for employees, none of the senior leaders actually cared, and neither did this bully boss.

Bringing our authentic selves to work can often be uncomfortable and challenging to do. Wikipedia defines authentic leadership as an approach that emphasizes building the leader's legitimacy through honest relationships with followers who value their input and are built on an ethical foundation. It goes further to say that authentic leaders are positive people with truthful self-concepts who promote openness.[5]

We thought this leader, who turned out to be a bully boss, promoted openness, only to find out later that he used his disingenuous inquiries about employees' families for performative reasons, not because he truly cared. After years of leaking confidential information employees disclosed and at other times outright speaking openly about private situations in front of other team members at dinners or social functions, people shut down and refused to share details about their lives out of fear of their personal details being shared. Everyone who knew of his behavior placed bets about when their personal details would be shared and with whom they would be shared. Would it be at an all-employee meeting? In the breakroom? Or in the hallway as other employees walked by?

Once affectionately known as "The Great Influencer" for his charming ability to get people to open up about personal details, he became known as "The Bully" and was most closely associated with stories of betrayal and shame. Everyone knew it, except him.

An authentic leader who possesses the ability to be vulnerable creates a sense of comfort, and employees will take risks, make decisions, and make mistakes without fear of reprisal. Creativity and transparency grow and will ultimately lead to an increased bottom line because team members will share their innovative ideas to make the business more efficient, responsive, and profitable. My thought about authenticity is that authentic leaders are strong enough to be vulnerable and wise enough to know that vulnerability does not make them weak.

This bully boss, dubbed leader, created an environment quite the opposite. And although he occasionally told employees about his personal life, no one felt comfortable speaking about theirs any longer, and rightfully so. Employees felt that management knew or should have known that confidential information was being used against them and nothing was being done about it. They were justified in these feelings. Employees questioned, "If other leaders knew but wouldn't help, why should we say anything else, ever?"

Bystander Effect

In 2019, the University of Maryland conducted a study about how the bystander effect affects the workplace. The bystander effect theorizes that people are less likely to help a victim when other people are present. The bystander effect tends to occur at work when employees fail to speak up because the people in charge should know what's going on.[6]

Employees who would once take on extra work and help without being asked would no longer do so. Employees who once spoke up about the things that were important to them no longer did. They knew the boss was fake, and they had no desire to see him win in this business. When other leaders in the organization finally realized what happened through months of digging, investigating, and observing, they brought it to "The Great Influencer's" boss's attention, but he refused to accept it as true. He was also a bully boss, not a leader. Specific examples and verifiable truths were presented to the boss's boss and the evidence was ignored. His boss refused to accept any of it.

Randolph-Seng and Gardner explored the connection between implicit and explicit self-esteem as well as individual and leader authenticity. In a later chapter, we will discuss how self-esteem issues can destroy an individual and an organization when a person is promoted to a leadership role but has never dealt with their deeply rooted self-esteem issues. Randolph-Seng and Gardner concluded that developing self-esteem is an important precursor to being an authentic leader.[7]

In another reflection moment, this boss lacked confidence on many levels, both personally and professionally. Being a chameleon is indicative of poor self-awareness and low self-esteem, both of which lead to the inability to be authentic—an important trait for effective leadership.

"No matter what you want
as a leader, if you haven't
established trust, your goals
will be difficult to accomplish."

——Dr. Lisa Lindsay Wicker

CHAPTER 5

First, Take a Look in the Mirror

Dr. Lisa Lindsay Wicker is an internationally recognized thought leader, best-selling author, motivational speaker, and entrepreneur. As a Human Resources (HR) professional with over three decades of experience, she graciously shared her advice and stories of navigating as a leader in HR, interacting with other leaders, and inspiring people.

Having spent much of her career in HR, Dr. Wicker's advice to leaders is to communicate, display the appropriate behavior, and build trust. She says, "First, without the proper level of communication, team cooperation will not come easily." Displaying appropriate behavior and having HR leaders hold other leaders accountable when inappropriate work behaviors are prevalent is the second piece of advice. Last build trust through your communication and behavior. No matter what you want as a leader, if you haven't established trust, your goals will be difficult to accomplish.

Striking a balance in knowing how much information should be communicated and when to communicate it distinguishes good leaders from those who are not so good. Stopping to ask yourself and your trusted advisors what people need to know and working with your HR team to create key messages will assist leaders with aligning their messages and decrease the chances of chaos and confusion.

Dr. Wicker holds herself, her teams, and the leaders she advises to high standards—and believes behaviors that align with truly authentic, transformational leaders should always be displayed. Examples of those behaviors are being open to new ways of thinking, having the ability to admit mistakes and to learn and grow from them, being willing to take informed risks, building trust through authentic and transparent communication, and moving forward in business—acting, not procrastinating. Dr. Wicker says, "The past is a prelude to your future. It sets you up for today and tomorrow. The past is gone and there is nothing you can do about it. If you are stuck in procrastination and stagnation, it's because you haven't moved on from the past. You are not experiencing the present of now and you are missing so many valuable lessons." She advises leaders to deal with the past issues that may cause them to be less communicative, less empathic, or even exhibit destructive behavior.

When CEOs and other C-Suite leaders respect their HR teams and understand that HR is a critical component to the organization's success, the team is then positioned to provide guidance and help drive the culture and norms of the organization. Dr. Wicker states, "There are three main components of an organization and those include: products, systems, and people. Products and systems do not work without people." Dr. Wicker has had the pleasure of working with Fortune 50 companies that get it. She adds, "Leaders in these organizations acknowledge that HR is a critical business component that serves as the foundation for the building to stand. They are unable to function without a strong HR team because if people are not functioning, products and systems are not sustainable."

Dr. Wicker and I both remember when HR was viewed as administrivia—paper pushers. HR should now be viewed as a strategic function. There are most certainly administrative tasks within the HR function, but when leaders are at the table making critical decisions about the future and direction of the business in six months, one year, and five years, the head of HR must be included at the table. They should have the opportunity to present people analytics and other data to make informed decisions and understand how people are contextually mapped across the organization now and in the future.

If HR is not connected to how the organization is evolving, there is no way they will ever be able to become proactive and strategic advisors. The role of the HR function should not be putting out proverbial fires and being reactive to organizational and human capital changes. Besides being an integral part of the team, HR must be allowed the autonomy to evaluate what is occurring outside of the organization to ensure they fully evaluate risks and environmental changes that could potentially affect the organization and people. By doing so, HR teams are able to efficiently and effectively deal with crises, such as "The Great Resignation," when they arise.

In one of Dr. Wicker's former companies, she led an initiative centered on employee enthusiasm. She pondered this initiative and how it could be carried out for such a large organization. After some time, she said to the leaders, "I know you have this idea that you can receive employee enthusiasm and that you can motivate them to bring it to work every day. That's not possible." She advised, "What we can do is start with us. As leaders, we must bring enthusiasm into the workplace every day and only then can we start a movement and change the face of the organization." Well, they did just that. Through a series of accountability measures, recognizing team members who displayed enthusiasm, and allowing team members' voices to be heard through a series of forums, surveys, and roundtable discussions, they allowed people to have a voice in what the organization's environment should be and how to drive towards it. Many ideas came from those discussions, but at the end of the day, it boiled down to such questions as: Who do I work for? Do I want to work for them? And can I be enthusiastic about it? Good leaders elicit affirmative answers to these questions.

For HR practitioners, putting such initiatives in place takes time and effort, but it can certainly be accomplished and sustained when we and our leaders are intentionally focused on authenticity.

Great leaders are smart about what they ask and know which battles to fight and which ones to surrender to. Surrendering should not be seen as a negative but rather as an opportunity to reflect, positively influence, and be intentionally focused on the next opportunity that is right for the company. Authentic leaders who are keenly aware of their abilities, the skills of their teams, and the capabilities of the organization know when to keep going and when to stop.

The final piece of advice from Dr. Wicker to all leaders is to take a look in the mirror first. Before they think about asking employees to consider the company's core values, leaders must ensure they are setting the tone, climate, and mood in the organization for the type of service and behavior they want displayed. It's one thing to have a core value on paper; it's another to expect team members to live that value. Leaders must start the movement—whatever movement they choose—by being the example.

CHAPTER 6

Leadership Law #2: Authenticity

Authentic leaders are consistent in their words and actions and certainly never hold situations against employees. Authenticity has a direct connection to trust and can be strengthened when leaders are open and honest. How great would it be to work in an environment where personal issues can be disclosed so that peers can support one another, opinions can be expressed, and employees can disagree without fear of retaliation?

There could be a gap between actually being authentic and employees having the perception that a leader is authentic. Finding a good balance is crucial for leaders to show up authentically, establish meaningful relationships, and maintain control of the organization. As Human Resources (HR) practitioners, we can foster authentic environments by encouraging small group meetings where consistent messages are disseminated throughout the organization and questions, as a result of the small group meetings, are shared with everyone.

When a question is posed by a particular person or group that the manager cannot answer, the question is given to the subject-matter expert to provide an answer. Each month, questions and answers are then provided back to all employees, which ensures consistency and transparency. Encouraging these types of meetings where talking points are created with input from all employees—including senior leaders and HR, and provided to managers—can be a starting point for authentic conversations. These small group conversations provide the platform for managers to spend time with employees to celebrate wins, discuss upcoming organizational changes, and other business without being afraid of not knowing the answer to a particular question. By encouraging the subject-matter experts to provide answers to questions managers may not know how to answer, we lessen the likelihood of managers "making it up as they go," thereby creating the perception that every leader must know everything in order to be a good leader.

I'm sure many of us have witnessed instances where managers are confident in their lies, so they make up answers that sound correct but in fact are not, and they leave their employees with wrong information. When managers and employees know questions will be answered by the subject-matter expert in their business unit or organization, they don't have to pretend to know all the answers and therefore it becomes normal to say, "I don't know the answer to this question, but I will forward it to the responsible person and we will come back to you with an answer." Simple, right? Not so much. This requires leadership buy-in and a leader who understands the importance of authenticity.

If you find that your organization is lacking authenticity, as an influencer and people expert, propose these types of meetings as a way to establish increased employee engagement and communication. Communication tends to be a problem in many companies, both small and large. By intentionally creating a structured platform for leaders to be authentic, identify strengths and areas of opportunity, and discuss business and a certain amount of personal sharing, this will set employees and the organization up for a successful future, all the while creating an authentic environment. Leaders should ask employees about their families, vacations, and hobbies without ever using it against them, as the bully boss described in chapter 4 did.

Employees bring unique attributes, backgrounds, education, and experiences to our organizations, and encouraging them to share their ideas and opinions will help build an environment where they can bring their whole selves to work. By being a positive example, we can inspire employees to share, even when they think their ideas are not important or may not be implemented. Ensuring that we and the leaders we support are sharing thoughts and ideas, some of which will be implemented and some of which will not, will demonstrate to our team members that we are all given equal consideration. This strategy helps stimulate creativity, increase innovation, and create a sense of belonging. Authentic leaders actively listen and can hear employees' ideas and, more importantly, care enough to act on them.

According to *Oxford Learner's Dictionary*, belonging is "the feeling of being comfortable and happy in a particular situation or with a particular group of people."[8] Also, Wikipedia says, "Belongingness is the human emotional need to be an accepted member of a group. Whether it is family, friends, coworkers, a religion, or something else, people tend to have an 'inherent' desire to belong and be an important part of something greater than themselves."[9] As HR practitioners, providing a safe environment where people can be their authentic selves is a duty that we can take pride in creating.

HR and departmental plans must align with the organization's strategy in order to be successful, which requires input from the employees and front-line leaders. I like to say, "To be successful, we have to row in the same direction, and we do so by knowing which way the captain wants to go." For employees to align their goals with the goals and strategy of the company, they must know what the strategy is, and it must be communicated properly. Leaders who listen to their employees' development goals and encourage their goals to correlate with the organizational strategy create transparent communication, authenticity, and a caring environment that extends beyond just getting the work done.

The Other Side of the Coin

Let's discuss the authentic jerk boss. Being authentic also means that we may sometimes deal with the boss who is not so nice, but they are authentic. I would prefer people to show me who they are so that I can deal with them accordingly. When a leader is rude, talks down to employees, and genuinely only cares about themselves, they clearly show they are not kind, but that is who they are. Who they are may not be who we would like to deal with, but they are being authentic, and we then can play with the cards we've been dealt. We always have choices, though, and we can decide to work with bully bosses. Should we decide to accept the challenge, leadership development can and should be employed.

According to Randolph-Seng and Gardner, leadership development programs designed to increase leader self-awareness to increase esteem may be useful.[10] Influencing leaders to understand the need for development involves intense listening sessions. Besides the small group meetings, deploying timely employee engagement surveys can assist in this effort. I often talk about engagement surveys and listening sessions because it is important to be aware of your team members' wants and needs to ensure you allot resources appropriately. If you don't have experts on staff, consider bringing in leadership development experts who can guide development. Doing so can make the process exciting, and your leadership development partners will collaborate with you to create a model to show the impact to the bottom line.

Leaders, especially those who really need it the most, will dread working on themselves and will find every excuse under the sun not to attend coaching sessions and workshops. I have found that leaders want the results from a good leadership development program but fight tooth and nail to not do the required work to yield those results.

To get buy-in, we should present learning possibilities as an opportunity to decipher what is needed for the overall organization. By doing so, those hesitant bully bosses will be more apt to engage. We could start by helping these bosses understand that authenticity is not sharing all of their deepest, darkest secrets, nor is it maintaining the status quo, especially when the status quo is not working. Admitting mistakes when solving an important problem and sharing facts without making excuses is authentic. Leaders are often put in sticky business situations that require swift decision-making. Great leaders aren't afraid to make decisions given the information that is before them, and they understand the risks involved in making quick decisions. Authenticity comes into play when the decision turns out to not be the most effective. Great leaders can admit when the decision they made may not have been the best one, and they do so without excuses. They are human too, and not without faults—and they are OK with that.

As I stated earlier, I had the pleasure of working with outstanding leaders and the displeasure of working with leaders who did not inspire others to work hard, who were not visionaries and were, simply put, bully bosses. When I worked with great leaders, our employees showed up ready to work and gave the business their all. We could settle our disagreements civilly because the leaders supported opinions and encouraged open dialogue that sometimes ended with "agree to disagree." Doing so did not make team members bitter or less willing to continue putting in hard work. They actually worked harder because there was balance and order within the organization. The leader was of the mindset that not all arguments are worth winning and it was reasonable to win some and lose some. That mentality resonated with us, and we respectfully battled out our ideas and still showed up authentically every day. We maintained the ability to work side by side with people we disagreed with the day before because at the root of the authenticity was a clear baseline of value and respect for each other.

It is important for HR practitioners to remember and remind leaders that employees don't want a perfect leader. They would rather have a flawed human being they can relate to but still feel admiration and respect for—so much so that they will do what is necessary to produce the work that is expected. Certainly, personal storytelling that reveals what leaders have endured and the lessons learned in their careers is salient in building authentic relationships, but no leader is required to bare it all. So, when we are dealing with a boss who is not authentic or who is an authentic jerk, let's start small and work our way up.

Understand that, as with other important cultural shifts, we will not all be able to start in the same place. We work in different organizations that value unique qualities and have leaders who are not all the same. Meeting your organization and your leaders where they are is crucial in making these types of initiatives sustainable.

SECTION

2

Authenticity Reflection Questions

1	Am I acutely aware of what behavior the leaders in my organization expect from all employees? What do they expect? Be specific.
2	Do the leaders in my organization show up genuinely and allow others to do the same? Provide specific examples.
3	Do the leaders in this organization show authentic concern for employees and the organization? Provide specific examples.
4	Are the leaders in this organization adding value to others and encouraging them to partake in being part of something greater than themselves? How is this being done? Be specific.

5	Do the leaders in this organization admit their mistakes openly and honestly? When have they done so? Be specific.
6	Do the leaders in this organization encourage employees to admit mistakes and do so without reprisal? Provide specific examples.
7	Have I witnessed the leaders in this organization encourage shared thinking versus siloed thinking? Provide specific examples.
8	Do the leaders in this organization need to prove that their point of view is the correct one? When have I seen them willingly accept other points of view? Be specific.

respect

"It's hard to see the
whole picture when you
are in the frame."

——Les Brown

CHAPTER 7

Wait . . . What Just Happened?

Have you ever been the subject of a humiliating situation and didn't realize that you were humiliated until later? You may ask yourself, "How is that even possible?" Let me explain . . .

After starting my Human Resources (HR) consulting firm, I established myself not only as an HR expert but as a speaker. A company that had not been a previous client reached out to me and asked if I would be interested in leading some onstage panel discussions. I immediately said, "Yes." Then they offered what I wanted more than anything—to be the keynote speaker for their event. I was elated just to have been chosen to take part in this event, let alone be the keynote speaker.

For at least six months leading up to the event, the team tirelessly planned the location and logistics for travel, accommodations, and meals. The sponsors and organizers diligently debated the agenda, workshop activities, and breakout sessions that would take place throughout the conference. Evening dinners, team-building activities, and every other detail you could imagine were thought through meticulously. The organizers for this company were charged with executing a conference for hundreds of employees from around the world, and every minute was intentionally organized.

The agenda was set, hotels were booked, and entire restaurants were retained and paid in full to accommodate the massive group. Finally, it was time to depart. I had not been a part of this team, but based on how every detail of the event was planned, this was definitely not their first rodeo, and I knew the experience would be amazing.

I Hate Squid

You heard about my love for a good meal in chapter 1. Now, let's talk about one food that I have tried many times, both domestically and abroad, and yet I still despise: squid. Now I tend to be open-minded about a lot of things, and I am always up for a healthy challenge. When I travel, whether for business or for pleasure, I explore exotic foods and generally love them. However, when it comes to squid, I hate it. Squid doesn't look so bad because chefs usually clean it up, filet it, and fry it to completely change the texture and look. But in certain regions of the world, squid is served in its natural state and it is genuinely disgusting—in my opinion. I do not want to offend lovers of squid, nor do I judge you. My statements about this particular cuisine are solely my opinion, so please, by all means, continue partaking of it without regard to my opinion, if you so desire. If I love a dish that another person finds disgusting, I am not offended by that at all and like to think of it as "more for me."

So, the squid from this little restaurant looked like they just pulled it out of the ocean, rinsed it off a bit, and slapped it on a plate. Little bits and strings from the insides of the squid remained when it was served. Enough of that. Just know it was disgusting.

Several people from this organization explored the city with me as we ate, drank, and got to know each other on a deeper professional level. I made it known that I would try the squid, but I was not fond of this dish. After reluctantly accepting the challenge, it was apparent that I was disgusted, and everyone knew it.

Showtime!

By building my muscle for speaking, after some time, talking in front of others came easy to me. I refer to building the speaking muscle because I tend to have some nervous feelings and butterflies when I'm speaking in front of groups, and I think that's normal for most people, but I can do so without being overly anxious. I built my confidence for speaking to large groups by simply doing it, despite the nerves. I never want to forget my first line, so I focus on it and I read it over and over to recall it word for word. The first line is so crucial for me, and I agonize over it because I know how important it is to nail it. Once that first line has been delivered successfully, I can breeze right through the rest of what I have prepared.

I was nervous when I was called to the stage to lead a couple of panel discussions, but not being the focus of the discussion took some of the pressure off as I prepared for day two. The first day turned out to be a normal conference day, and I would dare say most people felt pretty good about the venue, the food, and more importantly, the content.

The second day was the day. This was my time. I was reintroduced and called to the stage to deliver the keynote speech. The speech was well written and, if I can say so myself, delivered flawlessly. Cheers, applause, and being bombarded with welcomed questions and conversations at breaks and lunch was what I contended with for the rest of the day. I was elated and on a natural high because I remembered my first line and the speech was so well received.

Breakout sessions were engaging, and the information that was presented was informative and relevant. Participants were all in and fully committed to do what the company needed them to do for the remainder of the year after hearing energizing messages from the company's board of directors, leadership team, and expert consultants.

The organizers planned the third day as a half-day session to accommodate anyone needing to depart for home around lunchtime, as many of the participants would not arrive home until the following day. Much planning had gone into the event and workshops, and the leaders wanted to thank those who executed a flawless event.

To end the day with positive energy, one by one, leaders called the organizers of the event up to the stage and gave them extravagant gifts, handwritten thank-you notes, and congratulations for a job well done. Then it was my turn to receive my gift for serving as a panel moderator and keynote speaker. Excitement filled the room and positive energy was felt throughout the venue. I was excited—except I did not receive a note or extravagant gift. Instead, I received a plate of fresh squid. What's so sad is that the leader of this event knew I hated squid because we had explored the city before the event and had laughed and joked about it.

Until this day, I don't know if they really thought this gesture was comical or if their goal was to humiliate me. They tried to entice me to eat the squid on stage, but I refused. When thinking back on the entire experience, we had a great time throughout the conference. There were many funny moments and for me, this was just another joke, or so I thought. Mostly, everyone laughed along with us. We slapped a few knees, hit each other in jest, hugged as we walked offstage, and ended the well-orchestrated event.

I take my profession seriously, but I do not take myself too seriously, so I didn't bristle at the disrespect. At first it seemed as if the onstage squid was a harmless prank. We joked around with each other during our brief moments together, so surely the intent was only to lighten the mood after tackling such hard topics as developmental goals for managers, financial targets, and other expectations for the year. However, in retrospect, lightening the mood—if that was the intent—was at the expense of trying to humiliate me. So it was personal.

Being in the Framed Picture

I was disrespected at that moment, but I do not allow that incident to define me or make me question my worth and abilities. The crazy thing about it all is that I didn't even know that I was humiliated and disrespected until later. If you have ever been in an environment where everyone around you sees a situation one way and you simply cannot because you are in the middle of the particular situation, you understand that it's hard to see the whole picture when you are in the frame. I was focused and put in a lot of hard work, energy, and creativity into writing that keynote speech and delivering it, but it was overshadowed by antics.

I am positive that the substantial fee for attending a two-and-a-half-day event, flying first class, partaking of the finest meals, and lodging in a fabulous boutique hotel made participating much more palatable at the time, though. Regrettably, all the wonderful experiences and memories that were created during that trip continue to create mixed emotions for me. On the one hand, I was wined, dined, and earned a hefty fee for my work because I delivered good work. On the other hand, I was dehumanized in front of hundreds of people. Can you imagine how this entire experience could create such contradictory emotions?

I received apologies from various staff members via email and by text for quite some time after the event. The consensus was: the squid act wasn't funny; it was disrespectful.

Had I thought about what was happening in the moment, maybe I would have handled it differently—or maybe not. I could have whispered to the person who brought the squid on the stage right then and there, "This is disrespectful. Please take that off the stage." Maybe I would have cried if I thought about it too much. I really don't know how and why it all happened the way it did and why I responded the way I did, but I do believe things sometimes happen beyond our comprehension at the time to protect us. Taking the incident as a joke was the best course of action for me. I handled the joke, if it was meant as that, graciously and tactfully.

I realize now that a respectful leader with a positive regard for themselves and an acute sense of self-esteem would never have pulled such a stunt. I wonder now, all these years later, if the person realizes they may have some trauma to be addressed and, by doing so, they can make space to develop positive leadership characteristics and be a kind human being. I often think about what may have happened in their childhood that made them this way. Maybe their childhood was quite normal and they just grew up to be a bully. Who knows? But whatever the case was for them, I do hope that a colleague, loved one, friend, or foe has shed some light on their situation to invoke changes to their behavior.

"To be a great leader, you have to ask great open-ended questions, listen closely for the answer, and never anticipate what you think you know."

——John Costello

CHAPTER 8

Winning Together

I spoke with my friend and successful entrepreneur, John Costello, founder and president of Costello Real Estate and Investments, headquartered in Charlotte, North Carolina, about leadership, leading a successful organization, and how he and his wife have built such a successful real estate company in a relatively short period. They established Costello Real Estate and Investments in 2014, and it has become of the fastest-growing real estate companies in North Carolina, with offices in Charlotte and Raleigh, as well as Fort Mill, South Carolina. Costello currently employs more than 400 agents across North and South Carolina.

John attributes all of his growth and success to his team. "To be a great leader, you have to ask great open-ended questions, listen closely for the answer, and never anticipate what you think you know," said John. The most important aspect of great leadership for John and his wife, Natalie, are to lead with respect, empathy, and conviction. When the Costellos, as a unit, make decisions, they always consider how it affects the people who rely on them. Always!

I sent John a few guiding questions to ponder before our phone call, and once he had a chance to read them, he asked me if he could include Natalie or other members of his team on the phone call during the interview. His rationale for asking was that his partner and team members are integral in running the business, making decisions, and leading, so he wanted to invite them.

I thought in that instance, even when he can have his moment in the spotlight, John is thinking about everyone else. That was one of many reasons I was so excited that he agreed to the interview. Don't misconstrue my statement, I understand the power of a well-functioning, cohesive team, but for this project, I wanted to understand more about how an outstanding leader, who has been recognized as such in our community, thinks. I wanted his perspective because so many times I see leaders who are not respectful, who don't lead with empathy, and simply do not care as much about their employees as they do about themselves and/or the entity itself. John is the complete opposite of that.

"Winning Together" is the cultural compass John uses for big decisions that affect those he is honored to lead. John says, "All decisions that are going to possibly affect others must align with winning together. If it doesn't, that is not the right decision for the organization."

For John, winning is about engaging with collaborative, business-minded people who care about each other. He stresses that an abundance mindset, not a scarcity mindset, is an important aspect of the culture and of winning together because the team sets the tone for the culture, which he believes is massive in driving performance.

John says that he and Natalie ensure the policies and procedures of the organization align with the vision and mission to maintain the culture that they have built and are so proud of. "I believe that when the team sees how Natalie (he affectionately calls her Nat) stayed the course, they see us as our true selves, transparent and forgiving, and now everyone in the organization treats each other in the same way. Our forward thinking has become contagious, and now the team are all forward thinkers, open-minded, respectful of themselves and the team. The best has been brought out of all of us because of the way we show up daily."

When the agents at Costello Real Estate and Investments bring forth an idea that needs to be fleshed out a little more, the team rallies around them to help motivate and provide guidance and support. The leaders at Costello not only listen to their agents' ideas respectfully, but they expect them to have ideas and welcome them. Not every idea is implemented, but no idea is off the table just because of the way-we-do-things mentality. To continue growing as a business, pouring into agents so that they continue to grow and be leaders in the community, they carefully examine all ideas to ensure feasibility and that each idea is congruent with a winning culture. Unfortunately, not every organization will have a John and Natalie Costello at the helm. John and Natalie take feedback seriously. Having worked in the staffing industry, John respects the work of Human Resources professionals and knows the value of happy employees.

CHAPTER 9

Leadership Law #3: Respect

What happened to me on that stage in chapter 7 was disrespectful. Receiving squid as a gift for a job well done was not the first time I had been disrespected in my career, but I didn't have to work for that company every day. Unfortunately, others did. I was made aware later that similar instances occurred within the organization previously, which meant many team members were not surprised. They were disappointed, but not surprised. Some team members confided in me and said that they had spoken up many times about the disrespectful behavior people endured, but it didn't seem to matter much, and the behavior didn't stop. The HR representative for this organization was at her wit's end, too, because this bully boss was negatively impacting morale, which did not make her job of attracting, engaging, and retaining talent any easier.

As HR professionals, we are tasked with a fine balance of taking care of the organization that employs us and taking care of team members within the organization. Being the liaison between employees and their managers, keeping the best interest of the organization at the forefront, and balancing the needs of employees can be a juggling act. As we navigate our way through the organizations we support and for the employees we serve, we may become discouraged, disappointed, and even fearful that if our behavior is off balance, we lose the respect of the leaders or employees.

I think we can all agree that it is extremely important to create and maintain a positive organizational culture. The most glaring implication of not doing so focuses on attracting and retaining talent. If you manage a talent acquisition team, are responsible for attracting and retaining talent, or support managers who rely on you for doing so, you understand the impact a positive culture can have on securing talent.

Respect and creating a positive organizational culture involve much more than occasionally offering a free lunch or having an annual holiday party. Culture lives deep within an organization and can't be found on a poster in the break room or conference room. Wikipedia defines respect, also called esteem, as "a positive feeling or action shown towards someone or something considered important or held in high esteem or regard." Respect is a deep admiration for someone or something elicited by their abilities, qualities, or achievements.[11] Culture is how we do things, and it directly affects how work gets done, how employees interact with each other, and why engaged employees remain with the company.

You may wonder who is responsible for a respectful culture. Well, the truth is everyone is responsible for it. Essentially, though, a company's culture is a direct reflection of its leadership. Boris Groysberg et al. stated, "Executives are often confounded by culture, because much of it is anchored in unspoken behaviors, mindsets, and social patterns. Many leaders either let it go unmanaged or relegate it to HR, where it becomes a secondary concern for the business. This is a mistake, because properly managed, culture can help them achieve change and build organizations that will thrive in even the most trying times."[12]

Business owners, unless they are HR practitioners, rarely think about culture in the beginning, and I often remind them that they created their culture before they even hired their first employee. As they scale their businesses, the need arises to hire people, and without understanding how important culture is, they often handle people and culture in a haphazard, unstructured way. One day, the founder looks around, and the culture is much more complex than it was in the beginning. The company they built is now a mixture of values, attitudes, and beliefs of the founder and their leaders. Although they want to maintain the integrity of the business they fought so hard to build with their blood, sweat, and tears, doing so can pose challenges when the culture has not been evaluated in years. Mission and vision statements are often defined early on as part of the organization's foundation and, in order to attract employees who have similar beliefs and values, it must be clearly understood, communicated, and maintained. As an organization evolves and takes into account a shift in strategy or market demand, although rare, so might the mission, vision, and core values. However, overall the foundation of the organization is established and is based on the expectations of founders and leaders. Each of these essential elements of business must be visited regularly to ensure they remain aligned with a culture of respect.

If you have ever taken part in workshops or trainings, you know that even when a leader is not appointed to a group to solve a problem or work through options for a case study, a leader will always emerge. A notetaker also emerges, and members contribute to solving the problem. The same holds true in organizations. Natural leaders take charge when they feel it is necessary to do so. The actual leader of an organization holds the leadership title, such as CEO, president, vice president, and so on. A perceived leader may not hold one of the higher leadership titles, but based on their leadership actions, may be considered the leader by team members. If the leader, actual or perceived, sets a positive tone, we as HR practitioners have the pleasure of working with engaged, productive, and happy employees.

For sure, not everyone is going to be happy all the time, even under the best circumstances. But I am optimistically hopeful, so I believe that most of the time situations will be resolved in the best possible way and will impact people in a positive way. This does not mean that I walk into every scenario with rose-colored glasses, thinking that all is well with the world. I understand, however, that organizations with mostly happy people will see an increased bottom line because productivity will extraordinarily increase and people would never want to experience anything differently.

On the other hand, if the leader, whether actual or perceived, sets a negative tone, we as HR leaders contend with disengaged employees, high turnover rates, or even worse, employees who remain employed and mimic the bad behavior of the boss. They wreak havoc throughout the entire organization. For instance, if those in charge in an organization behave in a passive-aggressive way and manage as such, that passive-aggressive way of communicating and managing will pervade throughout the entire organization, because how could it not?

The results of a negative corporate culture and lack of respect for teams within an organization can be devastating to the business and its employees. When a company lacks a positive, strong, well-defined culture and leaders who can drive the company's mission, vision and values, the result will be employees who show up for the paycheck only. They come to work to maintain their livelihood, and for the time being, showing up is solely based on the exchange of money for their time. At some point, the paycheck will not be enough to keep them driving in to work every day, and those valuable, knowledgeable, and once fully engaged employees will leave.

If your work environment is not as open and respectful as that of the Costellos, mentioned in chapter 8, what can you do when your feedback and opinions are not taken seriously? How do you convince leaders of the importance of always striving to do the right thing when they don't truly value the HR function?

We have options, and we need to be creative in our approach. Having spent twenty-five years in corporate HR, I completely understand that it's difficult to speak to senior leaders about employee concerns, especially if those leaders are causing the concerns. However, we play a vital role in driving the culture of our organizations, so we must find a way to speak up.

To help drive a positive culture, we can welcome feedback from our employees and act on it. Employ a third-party vendor to administer an employee engagement survey or create your own. When we collect feedback, we must ensure that leaders understand what the real employee concerns are and address those concerns in a timely manner. When we have what we want to convey in writing via the survey, that is data we can use to present our case for driving change.

Bring facts and figures to the table when addressing team member concerns. Engagement surveys—barring you are asking the right questions—along with the presentation of opportunity costs, turnover costs, and low engagement and efficiency costs, are effective in demonstrating how the bottom-line numbers are impacted when we do not function within a culture of respect.

We, as HR professionals, can help to ensure leaders consistently communicate the same or similar messages to employees and that we all communicate often. Providing coaching, using metrics, making leaders aware of the negative behaviors that exist, and, more importantly, showing how those behaviors affect the entire organization can be a great start to building a culture of respect.

SECTION

(3)

Respect Reflection Questions

1	Is every person treated with dignity and respect? If so, in what ways have I witnessed it?
2	Does every individual have the opportunity to contribute to important conversations in the work environment? How are they invited to contribute?
3	Is active listening a part of our behavioral expectations? If so, when have I witnessed it? Have I ever witnessed certain people not being allowed to speak or share their ideas? When did this happen, and what were the circumstances?
4	Do the leaders in my organization value diversity of ideas and thought in background, education, and experience? Have I ever witnessed a time when diverse ideas and thoughts were not valued?

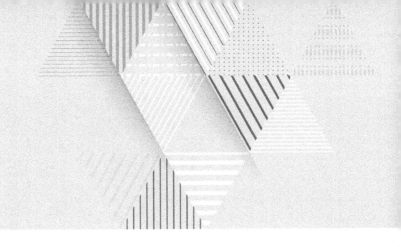

5	Does this organization respect employees as well as customers, vendors, partners, and the community? Have I ever witnessed disrespect towards any of these groups?
6	Have the employees in this organization been able to thrive in their careers, and are they able to contribute as individuals and within a team? Are there examples I can provide as proof of this statement?
7	Are managers and leaders consistent in the way they show respect to everyone? If so, when have I witnessed it? If not, when have I witnessed inconsistencies, and how can I address them with the leaders?
8	Has this organization created a baseline of what respect is and what the expectations of respect are, and is everyone in the organization aware of the expectations? If so, how has it been communicated, and how is it being lived every day? If not, how can I address it with the leaders?

emotional
intelligence

"There is an old-fashioned word for the body of skills that emotional intelligence represents: character."

——Daniel Goleman, 1995

CHAPTER 10

Insecurity—the Assassin of All That Is Beautiful

Content warning: this chapter contains references to rape and sexual assault.

When I met—let's just call him Sawyer—he and his beautiful wife had been married for twenty-one years and they had four adorable children. Their two boys were sixteen and fourteen years old, and their twin girls were eight years old. Sawyer shared a gorgeous eight-thousand-square-foot home with his wife, children, and their two dogs. He was living his dream life, seemed to have it all, and was on top of the world. He had a lovely wife who adored him, four children who idolized him, a huge seven-figure salary, and a high-powered job. Sawyer climbed the corporate ladder all the way to the top, and he was now CEO of a large architectural firm. Business could not have been better. He had grown the business from very humble beginnings with just shy of forty employees to a multimillion-dollar organization employing over one thousand architects and staff. Sawyer had led his team and the company to success and the stakeholders loved it.

They loved the revenue that the firm was generating, and they loved him. Sawyer had it all—or did he?

What Sawyer's employees, closest friends, and even his family did not know was that he was extremely insecure. He was insecure about many parts of his life, both personal and professional. He was insecure about his ability to maintain the comfortable lifestyle he had built for himself and his family, and he was insecure about his ability to continue maintaining the profit levels the firm's stakeholders had come to expect. The pressure to produce consistent growth year after year had weighed heavily on Sawyer, and he was unsure of how he could continue. He was getting older, and when he looked in the mirror each day, he saw an old man who questioned his abilities to keep up with life and work. He often questioned whether his wife loved him as much as she said she did, and he questioned if his children truly respected him. As the leader of such a large organization, he often debated with the thoughts he created within himself and lived with a sense of tug-of-war about whether his staff liked, respected, and wanted to follow him, or if they did so because of his authority and status. Sawyer didn't know if people were disingenuous or not, and he was constantly questioning it in his mind. He knew that his success in business influenced how people viewed him, but how many of his relationships were real and how many were solely based on his success?

The Darkness Behind a Bright Future

Sawyer's immediate family knew that he was bullied in school, but his wife, children, and most certainly no one in his firm knew of this. I'm sure we can all imagine what bullying does to the psyche, whether we have endured such bullying behavior directly or indirectly. Sawyer could never seem to get past the horrible names he was called, being pushed around, and the disrespect he suffered from elementary school all the way through high school. Sawyer was not fortunate enough to be born with the straight teeth, thick hair, or any of the overall features once considered the possession of the most handsome men by society. He was quite thin, awkwardly tall, and particularly pale. Sawyer once told me he felt his skin looked transparent sometimes, especially after a freezing winter. After being teased for so many years, as an adult, Sawyer was still insecure about who he was and how he contributed to his family, to work, and to the world, for that matter.

Sawyer's mother and father were farmers and were extraordinarily successful. The farming business survived four generations and was passed down to Sawyer's father, who modernized it with all the latest technology to remain competitive and maintain their family name within the marketplace. Sawyer's powerful family name carried a lot of weight in their community because they owned hundreds of acres of land, supplied reputable produce in almost every store in America, and were highly visible in government for their stance on land conservation and sustainability.

Despite the successful family business that had been passed down several generations, Sawyer decided early on that he wanted to move away from the region in which he grew up and called home to become an architect in a larger city. Sawyer was sure that as his parents aged, his sisters and brothers could operate the family business without him. He reassured the family that he would be available for advice, would help make decisions about the business when it was necessary to do so, and would visit often. Sawyer's parents and siblings supported his desire to move away and even encouraged it. He and his family knew, without saying, that he could leave their city and start a new life by leaving all the hurtfulness of being bullied behind. Sawyer's family inspired him and provided him with the comfort of knowing that limitless opportunities awaited him upon graduation from high school. They all knew that his decision to attend an out-of-state university was best. His family home was far enough away that he could distance himself from the horrendous bullying he endured for so many years, but close enough to maintain close bonds with his family.

Sawyer's family often overcompensated for his lack of self-regard by constantly telling him how great he was. They raved about what a great leader and role model to his siblings he was and how proud he had made them by obtaining academic success and multiple college offers. Sawyer felt great about his bright new future—but not about himself.

He eventually attended an Ivy League university and graduated at the top of his class. Upon graduation with a degree in architecture, Sawyer moved to New York, hoping to pursue his dreams of living life in the city and being employed at one of the top architectural firms in the country. Life in the big city wasn't easy, though. He had learned hard lessons about life as he navigated his way through multiple relationships and several dead-end jobs.

The one good thing that came out of working in restaurants in New York City is that Sawyer met the most fascinating woman he had ever encountered. Previously, he had been involved in many failed relationships, none of which he took very seriously anyway. But he knew that if this woman would have dinner with him, he would settle down. He knew from the minute he saw her that she would be his wife. He loved her exotic look, and he was drawn to her instantly. Well, he was smitten, and so was she. They dated for a few years and eventually married. During their years of dating, being married, and growing together, Sawyer landed his dream job in one of the most prestigious and well-known architectural firms in New York, which was no easy feat. He interviewed for roles within the organization and was rejected several times, but Sawyer persisted. After several interviews and thoughtful consideration, Sawyer's manager took a chance and hesitantly hired him. Once Sawyer was in the firm, he very quickly rose to the ranks of leadership and was making more money than he dreamed of.

Shortly after their marriage, Sawyer and his wife had their first baby boy and, about two years later, another boy. Sawyer was living the dream and even felt proud of his accomplishments. Sawyer always wanted a large family, just like he had growing up, so he convinced his wife after a few years to try again to grow their family. She so adored him and the life that he had provided for their family, so she agreed. After a few months, several tests, and a short stint in the hospital, the family found out that they were not only having one baby, but two new additions to the family, and they couldn't have been happier. Sawyer, his wife, and their two boys were elated to welcome twin girls into their nearly perfect lives.

During the birth of the twins, Sawyer got a glimpse of himself in the mirror, and he looked old. His wife was glowing, full of life, and was giving birth to two adorable creatures that they made together, solely out of the pure love they had for one another. In that moment, Sawyer put his head down and grabbed the top of his head with both hands as those feelings of inadequacy that he had felt as a boy came rushing back in like a freight train. He tried to forget, but could not escape, the feelings of the bullying he experienced so long ago. That day changed him. Inside, Sawyer turned into a small boy again and he could not shake the insecurity. He could not hold back the resentment he harbored toward life for dealing him such a bad hand. Sawyer no longer saw his life, his wife, or his children nearly as perfect. He instantaneously felt like an insecure little boy again and was no longer happy with his status at the firm, his wife, his children, and, more importantly, himself.

Insecurity Killed All That Was Beautiful

Because of his insecurities and unhappiness, Sawyer used his power as the CEO of the architectural firm that once thrived under his leadership to sleep with any and every female who was willing, and sometimes those who were not so willing. Sawyer had many affairs with women on his staff and one-night stands with women he picked up at bars across New York. He was incredibly careful to gain their trust by mentoring the women and applauding their efforts publicly and privately within the firm. Sawyer assured each of them they would have rewarding futures if they stayed close to him. He often made decisions without seeking advice from trusted advisors, which had not been the case before that fateful glimpse in the mirror during the birth of his twins and the nasty feelings of him looking old took over his thoughts. Sawyer camouflaged his insecurity with pure arrogance.

Once on a business trip to Washington, D.C., Sawyer and a female coworker worked on their upcoming presentations in her hotel room. She did not feel threatened by Sawyer in the least. Besides, they had worked together for many years, and she trusted him completely. Sawyer brought a bottle of wine and two glasses to her room, which she thought was perfect after a long day of travel and client visits.

They worked on their presentations, chatted about life and work, and sipped wine as they would under normal circumstances. This time, though, she did not know the night would end so horribly. It was not until Sawyer held her down on the bed and would not allow her to move that she realized she was in trouble. Sawyer thought she wanted this and rationalized in his head that she had even asked for it because, after all, she did willingly allow him into her hotel room. He allowed his insecurities to get the best of him and he made up in his mind that because he was a powerful boss in the firm, he could do whatever he wanted, when he wanted, and with whomever he wanted.

The firm where Sawyer was CEO was quite large now and had teams for every functional area, including Human Resources (HR). Unfortunately, many women had quit over the years and never confronted Sawyer or provided any indication to HR or anyone else about their real reason for leaving. Could it be that they were embarrassed, or maybe Sawyer threatened them?

For many years, other leaders noticed Sawyer was a different person than the one they knew before the twins. Sawyer had been a leader who collaborated and valued his team. He was not perfect by any means, but he respected others and he seemingly respected himself. After the birth of the twins, though, he changed, and no one knew why. Sawyer no longer made decisions under advisement; rumors swirled throughout the company about multiple affairs with women within and outside of the company, and he never admitted mistakes anymore. Team members would make other leaders, including HR, aware of some bullying behavior Sawyer exhibited toward them, but the other leaders did not take the complaints seriously and failed to address situations that could have protected employees. Senior leaders, including HR executives, did, however, notice that he no longer seemed to value their opinions as he once did. At times, there was a remarkable amount of turnover with no one ever knowing the true reasons, but it, too, seemed to have no direct connection to Sawyer.

Eventually, all of those brave women who had endured Sawyer's savage acts of violence came forward, and he was brought to justice. The lawsuits and millions of dollars his company paid to those women were never disclosed, but to this day, the company's name and brand are synonymous with turning a blind eye. Someone in that organization knew and did not intervene, or they should have known and stopped him long before he ruined his family's life and the lives of those women who trusted him. Sawyer's wife filed for divorce shortly before he was sentenced. She knew that her life and the children's lives would never be the same and they would suffer emotionally and financially because of her husband's actions.

This is an extreme case of someone not dealing with their insecurities and a toxic company culture colliding. Embedding organizational transparency as a way of being helps to establish a process of checks and balances and trust through open and honest communication. Transparency may not have completely changed the way Sawyer's insecurities manifested themselves, but there might have been fewer victims had there been some level of transparency that existed in the organization.

"Our society needs to
re-establish a culture
of caring."

—Nelson Mandela

CHAPTER 11

From a Results-Oriented Culture to a Culture of Caring

I spoke with John Ezzo, founder and CEO of New Image Building Services, established in 1988 and headquartered in Troy, Michigan, about leadership. I began working with John in 2003 and from my time at New Image, I knew that he not only valued Human Resources (HR) as a function, he also valued people, their work, and their differences. Even though life circumstances forced me to move from Michigan back to South Carolina, I dreaded having to leave such a wonderful organization.

Shortly after relocating back to South Carolina, I attended a leadership training and workshop in Atlanta, Georgia. Throughout the three-day workshop, we role-played, worked independently on case studies, and worked in teams to solve problems, demonstrate our leadership skills, identify gaps in our leadership style, and gather in-the-moment feedback that we could implement immediately to help enhance our leadership abilities. Over the years, I have attended many workshops, participated in many trainings, and have been certified in several leadership programs. But I vividly remember the workshop in Atlanta because the facilitator asked us to think about a manager for whom we had worked that embodied true leadership. My immediate answer was John Ezzo.

They then charged us with writing specific examples of the person's leadership style and why we chose them as our favorite leader. I emailed John shortly after that workshop to let him know about my newfound realization of him being the best leader with whom I had the pleasure of working. Back then, I didn't know the term "emotional intelligence" and certainly didn't realize that empathy was so important in leadership roles. Emotional intelligence is your ability to recognize and understand emotions in yourself and others, and your ability to use this awareness to manage your behavior and relationships. Emotional quotient (EQ) is generally represented by a score, like IQ, although there is no known link between IQ and EQ.[13]

When recalling the list of wonderful acts of kindness John showed me and my family, had I known the term at the time, I would have described him as emotionally intelligent and empathic. Today, not only do I know the term, but was so intrigued by it and the concept of it that in 2019 I became a coach and certified practitioner of emotional intelligence assessments.

John worked tirelessly on his business for many years and eventually expanded it globally. In 2016, while running his business in Qatar, tragedy struck. John suffered a stroke. A myriad of thoughts and questions ran through his mind: "What is going to happen to me? What will happen to my business? Will I make it back to America to receive the medical treatment I need? What am I going to tell my family? What will I tell my leadership team and employees?"

John returned to the USA for treatment and withheld his medical condition from his entire team—initially. He traveled extensively, and even though he was back in the USA, it wasn't uncommon for him to not be in the office on a regular basis. Everyone who works with John knows he is always available by phone or email when they need him. John was back in Michigan for several weeks and received medical treatment but did not come into the office until he could physically do so without assistance, so that no one would know that he suffered a stroke. One might immediately think that it was selfish that he didn't tell his team or that he didn't trust them. His reasons for not telling his team were just the opposite.

John stated, "I didn't tell my team because I didn't want to alarm and panic them. I didn't want to make my team's lives more difficult. I did not want them to worry about me, and I didn't want them to have to dispel rumors about my condition or wonder how to handle client inquiries should the news spread." John said that when he was physically able, he would use a private office and ensure the door was closed most of the time to limit the number of visitors and interruptions until he felt good about his health again. When we talked about culture, he explained that because of the stroke and when the staff was finally informed about his condition, New Image Building Services shifted from a results-oriented culture to more of a caring culture.

I would argue that they always had a culture of caring, but they elevated the caring culture to a higher level. For instance, John has always invested in training employees, but as a part of this shift into a caring culture, he began investing in development. The team provided input for what they felt they needed as a leadership team and John hired my company, HR Unequivocally®, to provide a series of developmental workshop opportunities for personal and professional growth.

Shifting to a learning organization that sought to increase an employee's overall effectiveness—in life and on the job—is just one example of how New Image cares more deeply for their employees.

We will talk about culture shifts later. In the meantime, let's dig deeper into how much emotional intelligence and empathy play a role in how an organization functions.

CHAPTER 12

Leadership Law #4— Emotional Intelligence

Leaders who have integrity and live by a set of moral codes would never display the same or even similar behavior as Sawyer of chapter 10.

Have you ever encountered a similar situation, in which a leader who once displayed exceptional leadership skills falls into the power trap and you notice but don't think it is as bad as it appears? Have you joined a company and this type of situation was apparent from day one? What did you do? How did you protect the employees, the company, and yourself? You may ask yourself how you could have done anything when no one gave a real reason to believe anything was abnormal. How could an entire team of Human Resources (HR) professionals in a large organization allow the type of behavior Sawyer displayed to go on for years?

There are many ways to overcome insecurities in leadership and in life when a person is aware enough of themselves to commit to a change. According to the Rosenberg self-esteem scale, although individuals with fragile self-esteem respond to self-report measures of self-esteem with positive evaluations of self, their self-esteem crumbles when they are confronted with challenges that elicit ego-defensive responses.[14] In laypeople's terms, a person can assess themselves as having a high level of self-esteem until they are challenged. When the person is challenged, they cannot defend themselves, so they lash out negatively, generally attacking the person who challenged them rather than defending the point that is being questioned. This type of person feels confident until the very moment someone disagrees with them, and then all hell breaks loose. Their insecurities are then revealed at a level that they had never experienced nor anticipated. They were not ready for someone to question them—and how dare they?

Race, age, socioeconomic status, ethnicity, religion, or anything else that defines us as individuals does not exclude the existence of insecurities. Imagine this: You are financially privileged and have all the means to purchase all of your heart's desires. You didn't earn the wealth; you were born into it. People who weren't born rich but earned it through hard work and sacrifice may make you feel insecure. This could weigh heavily on a person, and when they are challenged, their insecurities rear their ugly heads.

Let's be real. HR has a poor reputation in many companies, and there are many explanations for it. In a 2017 survey conducted by TeamBlind, five top-market firms reported their percentage of employees who don't trust HR as painfully high, with Apple reporting 72 percent, Amazon at 76 percent, Google with 72 percent, and Microsoft at 71 percent. The best performing firm was LinkedIn, with 59 percent of its employees not trusting HR.[15] This is heartbreaking!

Perhaps the reason for this terrible reputation is that some HR professionals just "fell into" their career and may find it difficult to own the role in the beginning. If this is the case for you and possibly you have not fully embraced your HR role, you have taken a major step in reading this book. I appreciate you learning from my experiences and from others who have been in the HR profession for many years.

I grew up in HR, received formal and informal education in it, and haven't wavered from the field since I started at age eighteen. This alone doesn't make me the perfect HR practitioner by any means, but I know a thing or two about HR. I have successfully handled court cases, managed in harsh conditions, laid off massive work forces, hired in the best and worst of times, supported senior leaders, and have had mentors and educators who poured into me during the past twenty-five years I have spent in the profession.

We have the inherent duty to protect the company and its employees, which is a delicate balancing act, to say the least. As we navigate our way through the organizations we support and the employees we serve, the balance can sometimes be misconstrued as uncaring, but in most cases, this couldn't be further from the truth.

HR practitioners have a tremendous amount of influence over our organization's culture simply because of the nature of our roles. To help influence the attitudes and behaviors of our leaders, we must suggest and provide training and introduce workshop concepts that may have otherwise not been taken seriously. We won't always be fortunate enough to work with someone with as much empathy and sound emotional intelligence as John Ezzo, mentioned in the preceding chapter, so we must be creative in influencing our leaders to understand the importance of developing empathy.

In the case of Sawyer, he most certainly could have and should have undergone intensive and ongoing therapy throughout his life, which may have yielded a different ending for himself, his family, and his career. I am not remotely suggesting that we, as HR professionals, can solve Sawyer-type issues within our organizations, but we can use our voices to do all that we can to protect employees. There was probably not much anyone could do with Sawyer, but we can recognize unacceptable behavior and educate our employees to recognize and report it, when and if they witness or experience it. Oftentimes, we are afraid of losing face or, more importantly, losing the means to support ourselves and our families, so we don't take complaints to the highest-ranking individuals, groups, or boards within or outside of our organizations. We have an obligation to protect the company and the employees, even when doing so makes us uncomfortable.

As leaders in an organization, especially HR leaders, we are attentive in our pursuits to recruit, hire, train, engage, and retain the best talent. Somewhere in that list lies the strategic part of HR, and in our pursuit to be strategic, we must not forget about the humans in our HR processes.

As a certified emotional intelligence practitioner, my choice for assessment models is the Emotional Quotient-Inventory 2.0® (EQ-i 2.0) used by Multi-Health Systems Inc. (MHS).[16] MHS is a leading publisher of scientifically validated assessments and has produced a line of talent assessments that specialize in emotional intelligence, entrepreneurship, risk tolerance, and meeting facilitation.

I appreciate all aspects of the comprehensive nature of the EQ-i 2.0 model. I was so impressed and became certified by this organization for many reasons, but partly because of the reported well-being indicator that is an aside from the EQ score. This well-being indicator is used to measure a person's level of happiness, which could result in additional developmental opportunities. I believe that a person's overall well-being is an essential part of leadership. Finding the right balance in work and life and never wanting to jeopardize either can in and of itself cause stress. I believe that life is about balance, and one can be at peace when balance exists.

True leaders will use their power innocuously and will find balance to try to ensure that those around them do the same. They balance by protecting their time, recognizing when they need to address situations with unpleasant people, and promoting well-being throughout their organizations. When a leader is not balanced, neither is the organization nor the employees.

In addition to the important well-being indicator, MHS's EQ assessment is comprised of the following five scales and fifteen subscales:

1. Self-Perception
   a. Self-Regard
   b. Self-Actualization
   c. Emotional Self-Awareness
2. Self-Expression
   a. Emotional Expression
   b. Assertiveness
   c. Independence
3. Interpersonal
   a. Interpersonal Relationships
   b. Empathy
   c. Social Responsibility
4. Decision Making
   a. Problem Solving
   b. Reality Testing
   c. Impulse Control
5. Stress Management
   a. Flexibility
   b. Stress Tolerance
   c. Optimism

Source: MHS website: https://storefront.mhs.com/collections/eq-i-2-0

Don't get me wrong. I don't think that implementing workshops based solely on this model, or any other model for that matter, would have completely solved Sawyer's insecurity problem. Insecurities that run so deeply would most likely require more serious support and certainly more than group workshops. I believe, though, that employees, other leaders in the organization, and possibly even Sawyer himself, may have grasped the EQ concept and what it means to people and organizations if more were done. By introducing this concept and declaring its importance, leaders would have understood that everyone has deficiencies in some area of their EQ, and they would have realized that the good news is we can do something about it with intentionality. When the team realized they can increase deficient areas by taking notice and introducing strategies to purposely increase EQ, they most likely would have been open enough with one another to have truthful conversations about the observed change in Sawyer's behavior.

Had emotional intelligence data been conveyed throughout the organization by requiring team members to attend workshops, most would have understood this concept and subsequently put measures in place to increase their EQ with guidance and support. The senior HR executives who made recommendations to Sawyer in the years prior to his behavior shift may have been able to present him with data and real-life examples to help him realize he was spiraling downward and may not be able to recover if extreme measures were not employed immediately. The HR leader may have been able to show support and help the team realize that by protecting themselves, the organization, and their most important asset—people—they could have possibly avoided such an astronomical crisis. This type of mindset shift doesn't happen overnight and takes thoughtful planning, communication, and orchestration. By soliciting management buy-in and developing a proper plan for monitoring and sustainability, most of the team could have grasped the concepts and begun to be more aware of themselves and others.

As HR professionals, we sometimes get discouraged about speaking up for what we know is right out of fear or because leaders sometimes disregard our opinions, especially when there is no data to confirm what we are saying or proposing. Leaders tend to want facts and data, even when it comes to how employees feel. So, we must find a way to deliver facts and data, and we can do so by encouraging ongoing feedback through employee engagement surveys and other anonymous ways of gathering perspectives.

While reading the Sawyer story, I'm sure you thought that his impetuous nature and insecurities would eventually lead to his downfall. Not only did he ruin the lives of the women who were lied to and victimized, his family was ruined, and other employees in the organization who were aware of his actions were also impacted. The reputation of the company, other leaders, and HR were all destroyed by this behavior and their lack of caring enough to report it and hold Sawyer accountable.

The lack of emotional intelligence and empathy in this extreme case may not be the answer. However, consistent training and empowering as many talented people in your organization as you can to trust your HR team enough to report inappropriate behavior they experience, witness, or hear of is a great start.

When we are strategic and proactive in our work, we recognize the warning signs of leaders who do not have a good balance and can put a plan in place to address it. Rome wasn't built in a day, and neither will someone's empathy and emotional intelligence, but there are measures we can put in place to address our overall concerns and maintain a sense of balance and well-being within our organizations.

Here are three suggestions:

1. Conduct a needs assessment and present data to senior leaders to gain buy-in for their support and participation in all relevant activities. This critical step is often overlooked and underestimated when implementing a company-wide initiative. Many of us in the field of HR have been empowered with the ability to "do what we need to do" for our employees, and we sometimes fail to remember that we must have proper support for the sustainability of our brilliant plans. Many of our leaders never actually participate in the training that our employees are highly encouraged to take part in, and then we wonder why initiatives do not have sustainability.

   We must align our goals and desired outcomes with our senior leaders' objectives to see change disseminated throughout the organization. When these objectives are aligned and each person understands they must also participate in the initiatives, employees trust and support that our true intentions are for the good of the entire organization. This information must be clear from the start, so that all team members—from the highest level executives to every individual contributor—are aware of the impact that the initiative will have on the organization.

2. Design the program, hire experts, and designate a group for implementation. I suggest starting with senior leaders. It is vital to establish a clear set of goals and metrics to evaluate the impact that the training has on the organization. After the assessments have been completed, feedback has been delivered, and workshops have taken place, time will be needed for participants to practice

their newly acquired skills. As I stated previously, this does not happen overnight, so the establishment of Key Performance Indicators (KPIs) to monitor changes is a crucial step in the sustainability of your training. What are the important changes you want to see as a result of the training? What behavioral changes do leaders want to see in their employees because of the training? What are the desired outcomes of the training for each group or individual? How will this be measured?

Establishing behavioral metrics is time-consuming and necessary to achieve significant measures to analyze and report to stakeholders. Stakeholders in this context would be everyone within the company. Understanding how personal, professional, and social competence training is improving lives and the overall organization is critical if you want this program to be sustainable in the long run.

3. Don't become complacent and let your brilliant plan to influence the growth mindset of your team and company die a slow death. We've probably heard this phrase from employees, "This is just another flavor of the month." Don't let your program become the flavor of the month. A program is more than a one-and-done training. A program is a series of training and workshops that assist with developing the necessary skills of leaders and behaviors of individuals that are important to growth and success.

For any training that you implement in your organization, develop a schedule to adhere to for you, senior leaders, and managers in each functional area of the organization to ensure discussions about the training happen often. Based on the scope and size of your business, this plan can take many different forms. You might highly encourage managers to review steps individuals have taken to increase their EQ in monthly or quarterly one-on-one meetings. As an HR team, you meet with managers monthly or quarterly to review what steps they have taken and check in with team members as well, so that everyone understands the importance of the conversations. From the information you gather, determine the most efficient and effective ways to facilitate ongoing conversations with your teams in order to obtain the desired information for reporting KPIs.

Creating developmental opportunities for employees is vastly important and should be given the time and consideration it deserves. Your program requires all the cliché things we discuss in leadership, like hard work, dedication, and a desire to see change. It is simple. It is not simplistic, though. This is how we protect our employees, protect our organizations, and build trust. We must truly embrace our roles because we have many responsibilities. Remember to always keep the *human* in Human Resources by supporting and building emotionally intelligent teams.

The following action plan is meant to be thought-provoking and provide a template to reflect on what is best for your organization. By answering the questions and being clear about what is needed for your team, you can identify the most important training to implement now in your employee development program. You can start with empathy and emotional intelligence or introduce it later, but include it. After answering questions at the end of each section, including this one, you may find that it unfolds over the course of months or years, based on your organizational structure, size, and employee development needs.

Emotional Intelligence Reflection Questions

1. Assess organizational needs
    a. How will I complete this task? Does my team possess the required skills to conduct a thorough needs analysis?
    b. What support, tools, and resources will be required?
    c. Why am I doing this?
    d. What are the expected outcomes?
    e. When will I complete this task?
    f. Date completed: _____

Assessing organizational needs for your talent is ongoing and should be revisited regularly to sustain developmental programs.

2. Design the training
    a. How will I complete this task? Does my team possess the required skills to design training?
    b. If my team has expertise in this area, will we design training completely, employ a third-party expert, or use a hybrid model to design training alongside an expert?
    c. What support, tools, and resources will be required?
    d. When will I complete this task?
    e. Why am I doing this?
    f. What are the expected outcomes?
    g. Date completed: _____

3. Implement the training

    a. How will I complete this task? Does my team possess the required skills to facilitate training?

    b. If my team has expertise in this area, will we facilitate all the training, employ a third-party expert, or use a hybrid model to facilitate training alongside an expert?

    c. What support, tools, and resources will be required?

    d. When will I complete this task?

    e. Why am I doing this?

    f. What are the expected outcomes?

    g. Date completed: _____

4. Sustain the training

    a. How will I complete this task?

    b. When will I complete this task?

    c. Why am I doing this?

    d. What are the expected outcomes?

    e. Dates ongoing: _____

Follow up on the training to ensure it sustains. When you move to the next training sessions, think about how you will incorporate the initial one and build on it. Don't forget about the initial education when you move on to the next phase.

You will most likely find that when you design a program and collect data throughout the assessment, design, implementation, and analyzation phases, your program may require a shift. If you realize your team needs will require changes to your program based on the nuances of new team members, a change of business objectives, or something else, begin planning the change immediately to effectively sustain your program. By not doing so, you may find that competing priorities will hinder your progress because you are shifting. Your program may change, but it does not have to fizzle out because you are unwilling to pivot. Take a deep breath, refocus, and make the changes.

SECTION

5

support

"Leadership is a way of thinking, a way of acting, and most importantly, a way of communicating."

—Simon Sinek

CHAPTER 13

Snakebitten

It was an unusually hot summer day in South Carolina. It's generally warm in summer months, but that day was particularly hot, humid, and eerily quiet in the office. In this particular business, we functioned in chaos, so the office was never quiet. Not organized chaos, just chaos. The lawn was being professionally manicured, pine needles were being turned and fluffed, some other crew members furiously blew freshly cut grass into the field across the street, and others precisely leveled shrubs using the most advanced equipment in the market. Our lawn was immaculate on this hot summer day, and it was still strangely quiet.

Lunchtime came and went, and at precisely 3:30 p.m., as hardworking employees who would have preferred to be anywhere else rather than the office on a Friday afternoon were winding down and were mentally and physically preparing to go home, a few of the leaders strolled in from a day of golf. They had a great day on the course, which may not have been as disgusting as it was if they had not been all smiles and reeking of alcohol and cigar smoke. We had been in the office the entire day, working and servicing internal and external client needs for the company, while a few of the "chosen ones" played golf.

We looked around in awe, and questioned in whispers under our breath, "Is this really happening?" They thought it would be a good idea to drive back to the office after basically taking the day off, as if no one would suspect where they had been. In hindsight, I now know they just didn't care. The audacity of it all was more than some employees could handle. So instead of becoming angrier and possibly saying something they would regret, they left. Employees began clocking out for their regularly scheduled shifts, and others who were scheduled to be in until 5:00 p.m. simply left for home because of the blatant disrespect they were being exposed to.

Can Someone Please Dial 911?

As employees began walking out of the building to get into their cars, suddenly, we heard gut-wrenching screams. Employees ran back towards the building from their cars with a look of terror on their faces. What could have happened so quickly? An employee was walking across the freshly manicured lawn to their car and was bitten by a snake!

We knew something needed to be done, we needed help, and so we stepped into action. As any trusted Human Resources (HR) advisor would do, I picked up the phone to dial 911 immediately to get an ambulance en route as quickly as possible. I planned to go outside to assist the employee and ask questions later, but I wanted to act as fast as I could to have emergency medical technicians on the way. Before I could let the operator know what my emergency was, the CEO snatched the phone out of my hand and ended the call.

In shock, I yelled at him in an attempt to get a quick answer because what had just happened made no sense. He insisted I call his holistic doctor to take care of the snakebite instead of calling an ambulance. We all shuddered at the thought of what could happen if the employee didn't get help quickly. He went on the explain that he could drive the employee to the holistic doctor and they would be seen immediately because of his prior relationship, the number of referrals he has provided, and so on. Can you imagine what I was thinking at this point as we looked around, appalled by what he was saying? The boss of our organization, who had been out golfing all day, smelled of alcohol and cigars, and used a complete lack of judgment by coming in to the office afterwards, was now telling me he could drive the employee to a holistic doctor.

I am not reciting this story to debate the merits of traditional and alternative medicine. Instead, it has everything to do with the lack of leadership and judgment of the day. Let me explain just in case there's a question. I believe that both alternative and traditional medicine have their place in the world, and people in need of medical care should have the option to choose the type of professional they feel most confident can help them. When the employee was bitten by a snake, though, and required immediate medical attention at his place of employment, that was not the time to debate it. We had established policies and protocols for handling emergencies based on our safety obligations, and I knew what our workers' compensation representatives might say about such a thing. They may have asked exactly what I asked, which was, "What the hell?"

I, of course, questioned the CEO's recommendation given the employee may have been bitten by a poisonous snake and the fact that the CEO had clearly been drinking, which would have put the employee at even greater risk. None of us knew at that time whether or not the snake was poisonous, but we certainly did not want to take a chance of not providing the proper emergency care swiftly. Copperhead snakes are found throughout North and South Carolina and were common in our area. Our office was located near a pond and heavily wooded areas—a perfect environment for those slithering reptiles to make their way through the parking deck, the parking lot, and into the pine needles. I was careful not to escalate the situation by accusing him of drinking, so instead, I spoke about the risks to the company. After stating my case multiple times in different ways, explaining possible company liabilities, having exhausted employees run in and out of my office asking what we were doing and when we should expect emergency medical services, he finally acquiesced and allowed me to call for an ambulance.

"My Ideas Are the Best!"

Sure, we could probably agree alcohol clouded this bully boss's judgment in that moment, but this example was just one of many scenarios in which lack of support for almost any idea that was not his own was rejected. I have other examples of when a lapse in judgment by him hindered the decision-making process, but I'll hold on to those stories for the next book. The CEO did not support the ambulance idea because, well, his idea was to drive the employee for alternative treatment and since it was his idea, it had to be the best one. By and large, the organization did not coalesce in a way that promoted an environment of collaboration anyway. We functioned in chaos, mainly because of the boss's inability to make rational decisions. Many of his decisions were grounded in emotions, lack of trust for anyone else on the team, and the overall knowing-versus-doing mentality that was ever so present in the business.

You can relax. The ambulance arrived at our location and the employee was ultimately taken care of by the experts for a non-poisonous snakebite. The downward-spiraling turn of events that day, which ultimately ended with an absurd argument about how to handle a snakebite, was the topic of conversation among employees for weeks. The lack of support from the boss was generally a discussion point, but when an event of this magnitude occurs, that alone is what everyone in the organization talks about until the next thing happens.

Support can be exhibited in many ways. It is most noticeable when leaders surround themselves with talented experts and then empower those experts to make decisions and mistakes without reprisal. Experts should be treated as such, trusted and supported with the right guidance and developmental opportunities to allow for growth. This type of support requires a strong leader who will suspend their own agenda and understand their team's point of view.

Simply put, this type of supportive leader shows empathy and is emotionally intelligent. A supportive leader helps create a supportive culture. As with other parts of what is valued in an organization, a supportive culture will trickle down. This trickle-down effect will foster creativity and innovation because teams will not be afraid of exploring new ideas and supporting each other to make them work. Support and empowerment operate at the highest level when they function simultaneously, and successful leaders know this.

"In football, you have offense, defense, and special teams. Human Resources is like special teams. Every game starts with special teams!"

—Herman Moore, former NFL wide receiver and current CEO of Team 84

CHAPTER 14

Win Together. Lose Together

A business owner who is fully aware of the power of support through empowerment is Herman Moore, CEO of Team 84 in Troy, Michigan, and a former wide receiver for the Detroit Lions. Having played sports at the highest level, he recognizes there comes a degree of discipline most people will never realize. Herman understands that when a team member is not as strong in certain areas but leaders have created a culture of support, there will always be others that step up and do more to fill in the gaps. This level of teamwork and practice of support is not to overcompensate for shortcomings, but to allow team members the opportunity to be successful in their area of expertise as well as enhance and grow their skill set. This mentality is, as Herman says, "We win together. We lose together."

Ensuring standards are set and clearly communicating those standards is key to his success as a leader. I was fortunate enough to witness this culture in action when I visited the Team 84 headquarters. The team dynamic with Herman and his wife and business partner, Angela Moore, was fascinating. Witnessing how a transparent, authentic leader interacts with their team members is something I crave to see more in businesses.

Employees at Team 84 are happy, they are empowered, and they have fun! Empowering team members to make decisions and being supportive of them has allowed for a sense of freedom and given them the ability to challenge themselves to do and be better. Team members know they are not in the organization to take commands. They all have a playbook, and how much they receive is determined by how much they are willing to put into the team. Herman compares this level of freedom and support for employees to the level of commitment a team member puts in during practice when preparing for a professional game. Members of the team could choose to run fast each day or not; the choice was theirs to make, and it is the same in his business.

Employees, consultants, and team members are in control of their upward mobility and growth within the company with salary or position. Herman does not define it; the person defines it, and everyone is aware of it. He provides a blank canvas so that each person can own their part of the business and, subsequently, what the individual attains depends on their level of hard work and commitment. Herman provides as much support as they need to achieve their desired outcomes.

Herman's leadership style is to lead by empowering and supporting employees' growth through operating with transparent business practices. He analyzes the numbers and his team members are afforded the opportunity to see the bottom-line numbers to ensure everyone is aware of the financial standing of the company. He feels that this type of transparency has led the team to be as supportive of Team 84 as he is of them. Everyone respects each other. They listen to each other. They ask questions and all expect answers. It is amazing how employees operate at such a high level when a common goal is agreed upon and a shared purpose is pragmatic enough for everyone to adhere to.

There were so many gems that I gleaned from the interview with Herman, but selfishly my favorite part was when I asked who drives the culture. His answer was this: "The Human Resources department is the heartbeat of the company. We are people and they help establish the culture, mission, and expectations. People are not optional; they are mandatory, and we need HR because people *are at the center of* who we are!" In football, you have offense, defense, and special teams. Human Resources is like special teams. Every game starts with special teams!

Creating a culture of empowerment does not mean that individuals don't have boundaries and, from time to time, have to deal with their ideas being challenged. The culture at Team 84 is not one of rejection. Rather, it is described as challenging ideas to determine if the solution is really the best one. Herman stated he will mitigate risks as much as possible, all while providing the necessary support, resources, ideas, and feedback if the team member is adamant about an idea. It brings him joy to see employees thinking about out-of-the-proverbial-box ideas and working toward their goals with the best interest of the organization at the forefront of their ideas.

Another quote Herman lives by is that, as in the game of football, "'*L*' is not for losses, it's for lessons." He never wants his team to focus on the negative in ideas that are presented and tried, or on opportunities that do not yield the results they expected. Rather, he wants them to focus on the positive experiences from trying something new and the lessons learned from challenging themselves to think beyond what their instincts would have led them to do. We ended the conversation with him reiterating that engaging in the conversation with me about his team was reassurance that he is doing what he says he is doing in life and in business. Herman Moore is walking the talk!

CHAPTER 15

Leadership Law #5: Support

Successful businesses don't just happen. Leading a successful business takes resilience, flexibility, dedication, and, more importantly, building an engaged team. Successful businesses are generally not bereft of transformational leaders, but rather they possess a team of inspirational leaders who understand the importance of supporting employees. Supportive behaviors include acting with integrity, both personally and professionally. It is important for a leader to be consistent in their behaviors, and although we may not know all about our leaders' personal lives, I would dare say that someone who is supportive personally will also be supportive professionally. A supportive leader who leads with integrity is integral in managing a business and staff, making decisions with the best interest and the greater good in mind, and interacting with colleagues and clients. Successful leaders also give employees the authority to make decisions, challenge the status quo, and own their work.

Leaders who support their teams build on their strengths and will understand, accept, and act on their identified areas of opportunity. No one person can be the expert in all things business, which is why genuine leaders surround themselves with experts that complement each other's strengths and close identifiable gaps in the business and with teams.

As in the case with the snakebitten employee in chapter 13, the boss of the organization could have lessened the confusion by allowing me, the Human Resources (HR) director, to take the lead in the situation because there was much more to consider than what he saw on the surface. Protecting the employee and ensuring that he quickly received medical treatment was undoubtedly the most important first step. Ensuring that the company followed the rules as prescribed by its written policies, procedures, and the agreements made between the company and its partners, namely workers' compensation in this case, is also part of the HR function.

Being supportive does not mean that a leader should not question the status quo. I would be making inconsistent statements if I say that employees should be allowed to challenge the status quo without reprisal, while leaders should acquiesce to spare their employees' feelings. No, what I am suggesting is that a self-aware, supportive leader would hear the experts' reasons for making a particular decision or bringing forth a new idea, and then make suggestions to think through the idea or decision to encourage a degree of openness and vulnerability.

Understanding the knowledge, skills, and abilities of team members and building around that understanding is a reflection of support. As HR professionals, we can establish practices that promote two-way communication, which will often assist us and the leaders we support with gathering information about what motivates employees to achieve their highest levels at work. We can help them seek out the knowledge of talented employees and acknowledge their value by providing opportunities for team members to identify their strengths.

In our practices, whether through creating a structured performance management process or creating several types of mentoring programs designed for multiple levels, we should align our programs with the organization's needs and properly communicate these structures to our leaders and employees.

Another important aspect of building on the strengths of others after the establishment of such programs is to hold everyone accountable for participating in the work. When our HR programs align with organizational goals, we can clearly articulate the business case for all to engage in the process. When we can successfully communicate what the outcomes and benefits will be, that is a net win for leaders, employees, and HR. We create systems that ameliorate lack of support and allow individuals to understand how they support team and organizational goals. A climate where employees can openly give and solicit feedback, engage freely in developmental conversations often, and stretch beyond what has been traditionally accepted is an inviting professional support approach. By creating supportive internal systems, our teams can fully understand the broader business view and demonstrate how their skill set contributes to it.

Leaders can inspire their teams to do more when they are intentional in their actions and walk the talk, as Herman Moore does in chapter 14. They certainly do not show up on a Friday afternoon after not being at work all day, smugly talking about playing golf, and expecting that anyone will want to do more. This type of intentional disregard for employees causes low morale and lack of engagement, which ultimately leads to attrition. I state often that providing data and statistics to our leaders is one way to gain buy-in for our ideas.

You may wonder how you can gain the support and respect of your bosses when they have traditionally not been supportive or respectful. Leaders sometimes exhibit traits from the latter years of the generation before them and traits of their own generation, and they are, in many cases, leading a new generation they are trying to make sense of and attempting to support. That explanation, of the generations, can help HR professionals explain some of their leaders' behavior.

On the other hand, when garnering support from the unsupportive, we have to remember that, unfortunately there are bosses who are placed in roles and simply should not have been. They sought out leadership roles because they were expected to do so. They excelled in their area of expertise and were placed in a leadership role because of their high level of performance as an individual contributor, or a family friend brought them along as a favor while praying they would eventually embody leadership characteristics through maturity, self-awareness, and perseverance.

We have most likely encountered at least one of these cases and know it all too well. We realize later that they are not supportive of HR because hiring an HR professional to support the team was only a performative, check-the-box exercise. It looks good on paper to have HR. They should have HR guidance and therefore they bring in an HR expert. That type of bully boss has no clue how to support or manage people and has no desire to learn to do so effectively.

Now, the boss that I described in chapter 13, the inebriated one who insisted on driving a snakebitten employee to a holistic doctor, was not very supportive of many of his team members, but especially those he considered nonrevenue-generating positions. We may have found ourselves reporting to a boss like this because we accepted a role in the company under the assumption that the decision makers and other leaders actually valued our expertise, only to discover later that the presupposition was far from reality. They're leading the team by the skin of their teeth already, so they are certainly not willing to invest in growing themselves, learning more about effective leadership, or understanding how to activate a supportive culture within their teams.

As HR professionals, we can approach the leader from a place of curiosity in an effort to truly understand the rationale behind their decisions or lack of support. Research the characteristics of the previous generation to understand what impacted their leadership formative years to provide comparisons of what was important and motivated them versus what is important and motivating to employees now.

Practice What You Preach

Often, the most difficult undertaking we can endeavor upon is to practice what we preach. Based on the sheer nature of the number of decisions that must be made, exceptions that must be accounted for, and the fact that humans fall short sometimes, we too can become frustrated and exhibit unsupportive behaviors from time to time. In these moments, keep the following support questions handy so that you can take a candid approach with an open mind to provide the support that you want to see. Writing things down brings clarity. When we are clear about our profession, what we are doing for people and the business, and why we want to create an environment where employees feel supported and empowered, we can remove ourselves for a moment and take an objective look in the mirror to determine our next course of action.

I am keenly aware that this may be easier said than done, but we have to continue a growth mindset and constantly work on ourselves to ensure we don't fall into the trap of functioning in the status quo. When we act as role models for the organization, we increase the chances that the leaders will follow suit and, with one team member at a time, begin living the supportive culture we desire.

Support Reflection Questions

1	Is this organization supportive of employees through enriching job characteristics, such as the creation of meaningful duties and responsibilities? Do the employees have the ability to provide input about how to carry out their duties and responsibilities?
2	Are growth and development opportunities consistently available to employees? Can I provide examples that support my statement?
3	Can employees make mistakes without reprisal? Can I provide examples of employees being coached after mistakes and their esteem being maintained in the process?
4	Are our insurance and benefits programs aligned with the needs of the employees? Can the employees utilize our programs without being made to feel guilty about using them?

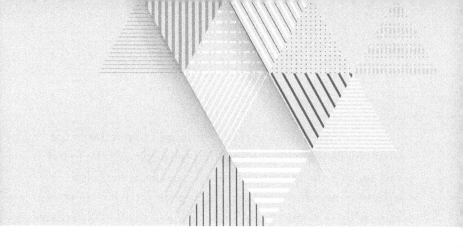

5	Are the employees' concerns heard and addressed timely by HR and other leaders?
6	Do the employees feel valued, emotionally supported, and psychologically safe enough to discuss difficult cases? Do I know this because we have conducted anonymous surveys in the last year?
7	Is collaboration among team members encouraged, and is time allowed for employees to understand how they work together? Can I provide examples of when our organization provided these opportunities?
8	Has this organization created a baseline for empowering employees to speak up and make decisions that impact their work? Can I provide examples of how this occurs in the organization?

CONCLUSION

As a Human Resources (HR) consultant to nonprofit and small, medium, and large for-profit businesses, I have found that most, if not all, organizational assessment roads lead back to none other than what we have been talking about—**leadership**. Conducting HR assessments, traditionally referred to as HR audits, and implementing sustainable, strategic plans are arguably the most important tasks organization founders can embark upon when their plan is to scale their business and hire employees.

Our mission at HR Unequivocally® is simple: "We partner with company leaders to create an environment where their employees feel safe, happy, and appreciated every single day." When leaders experience the power of happy employees, they will never want to lead from a different place.

Utilizing the CARES Leadership Model® program can be the difference in employees feeling engaged, empowered, and psychologically safe versus them feeling the opposite. When employees are disengaged, powerless, and don't feel safe, the organization experiences a loss of productivity, turnover, and the inability to attract new employees—all of which negatively impact the bottom line.

As HR professionals, we can help leaders examine the overall **C**ulture often, show up **A**uthentically, **R**espect themselves and others, increase their **E**motional Intelligence and empathy and **S**upport employees through providing data, understanding the importance of people, and using our voice even when it is uncomfortable to do so. Leaders need HR expertise within their businesses, and we need our leaders' support to help create environments we feel proud to support. There are so many nuances in leadership, none of which are mutually exclusive. And the varying characteristics leaders must embody and behaviors they should exhibit and maintain in leadership roles only add to the complexity of leading people and organizations.

As I am writing this book, we are experiencing the Great Resignation of 2021. Millions of workers in America are quitting their jobs, citing poor working conditions, lack of fair pay, and nonexistent work-life balance. Understanding the root of the problem is critically important to determine the resources needed for addressing employee turnover. Quantifying the problem through calculating your turnover rates and comparing it to previous years, conducting exit interviews to gather quantifiable data, and conducting questionnaires to ask your current employees what they need, can prove effective in getting buy-in from your leaders to develop a strategic retention plan. A retention plan will need a budget and, therefore, buy-in from those who make financial decisions within the organization. This is a first step in addressing the Great Resignation. But even with a strategic retention plan, if your company leaders do not value employees, are inconsistent in administering policies, and do not create a safe environment, no amount of data will help you stop the bleeding, proverbially speaking.

Low productivity is when employees are not using their skills and abilities to their maximum potential at work. According to a Gallup report collected from 195,600 employees and over 31 million respondents in the USA, poorly engaged employees with low productivity cost companies anywhere from $482 to $605 billion yearly.[17] Calculate the cost to your bottom line and observe who takes notice.

Navigating through the COVID-19 pandemic, being acutely aware of diversity, equity and inclusion as it all exploded in many organizations after the death of George Floyd in May

2020, and handling the daily business has required HR professionals to do more and be much more creative now than in recent history. Developing an attraction, retention, and engagement strategy, as well as handling employee relations, ensuring people are paid properly, coaching managers, being a strategic business, and mentoring among the other plethora of HR duties, are just the tip of the iceberg.

Each time that I begin to feel as if I am being overly optimistic in my thoughts about helping to create environments where everyone feels safe, happy, and respected, I recall HR Unequivocally's® vision: "To create a shared vision among enlightened, visionary, people-focused leaders who believe in the power of happy employees and always lead from that focus." Can you imagine partnering with a leader who genuinely wants employees in their organization to be happy?

I have always wanted to take care of people within organizations, and I always will, although now my primary responsibility as owner of HR Unequivocally® is to ensure that I am fully equipped and armed to equip others to take care of their people. I have the responsibility of growing this business and ensuring we fulfill our obligations to our customers, vendors, partners, and the community in which we serve and live.

What I learned throughout my time in corporate HR is that we must be flexible and be able to adapt to change quickly to survive. From 2020 to 2021, this lesson hit home in a major way when businesses shut down, employees lost jobs, and the COVID-19 pandemic turned our world upside down. Being flexible, adaptive, and always keeping our people at the forefront of our decisions keeps us accountable and ensures that we safeguard our businesses, but more importantly, it makes sure that our people are protected.

Team members are the lifeblood of any successful organization, as evidenced by the outstanding leaders that I had the pleasure of interviewing for this book and those not-so-great bully bosses I have encountered in years past. We have a moral obligation and a duty to protect our team members, and doing so means that we may have to voice an unpopular opinion when our leaders do not embody the characteristics and exhibit the behaviors we know are crucial in creating an environment that CARES about people.

To learn more about implementing the CARES Leadership Model® in your organization, contact HR Unequivocally® by visiting https://hrugroup.com or emailing TheLeaderWhoCares@hrugroup.com

ENDNOTES

1 Latin is Simple, "locum tenens," accessed September 22, 2022, https://www.latin-is-simple.com/en/vocabulary/phrase/1006/.

2 Google Arts & Culture, "Charlotte's Brooklyn," Levine Museum of the New South, https://artsandculture.google.com/story/kAWRQkCEYadDJQ?hl=en.

3 "Historic Charlotte Neighborhoods," J. Murrey Atkins Library, last modified August 21, 2020, https://guides.library.uncc.edu/c.php?g=621704&p=4626874.

4 Valerie Bolden-Barrett, "Study: Turnover costs employers $15,000 per worker," HRDIVE, published August 11, 2017, https://www.hrdive.com/news/study-turnover-costs-employers-15000-per-worker/449142/.

5 Wikipedia, "Authentic leadership," last modified June 20, 2022, 03:37, https://en.wikipedia.org/wiki/Authentic_leadership.

6 Phillip Nones, "The 'bystander effect' and how it affects our workplaces," Nones Notes, published January 5, 2020, https://nonesnotes.com/2020/01/05/the-bystander-effect-and-how-it-affects-our-workplaces/.

7 Brandon Randolph-Seng and William L. Gardner, "Validating Measures of Leader Authenticity: Relationships Between Implicit/Explicit Self-Esteem, Situational Cues, and Leader Authenticity," *Journal of Leadership & Organizational Studies 20*, no. 2 (May 2013): 214–31, https://doi.org/10.1177/1548051812464780.

8 *Oxford Learner's Dictionaries*, "belonging," accessed July 18, 2022, https://www.oxfordlearnersdictionaries.com/us/definition/english/belonging?q=belonging.

9 Wikipedia, "Belongingness," last modified June 26, 2022, 23:59, https://en.wikipedia.org/wiki/Belongingness.

10 Brandon Randolph-Seng and William L. Gardner. "Validating
    Measures of Leader Authenticity: Relationships Between
    Implicit/Explicit Self-Esteem, Situational Cues, and Leader
    Authenticity," *Journal of Leadership & Organizational
    Studies 20*, no. 2 (May 2013): 214–31, https://doi.
    org/10.1177/1548051812464780.
11 Wikipedia, "Respect," last modified July 15, 2022, 18:27,
    https://en.wikipedia.org/wiki/Respect.
12 Boris Groysberg, Jeremiah Lee, Jesse Price, and J. Yo-Jud Cheng,
    "The Leader's Guide to Corporate Culture: How to manage the
    eight critical elements of organizational life," *Harvard Business
    Review*, January–February 2018, pages 44–52, https://hbr.
    org/2018/01/the-leaders-guide-to-corporate-culture.
13 Travis Bradberry and Jean Greaves, *Emotional Intelligence 2.0*
    (San Diego: TalentSmart, 2009), 17.
14 Morris Rosenberg, *Society and the Adolescent Self-image*
    (Princeton, NJ: Princeton University Press, 1965).
15 John Sullivan, "HR, We Have A Problem: Up To 80% Of
    Employees Don't Trust Us," TLNT Talent Management & HR,
    published August 27, 2018, https://www.tlnt.com/hr-we-have-a-
    problem-up-to-80-of-employees-dont-trust-us/.
16 See https://storefront.mhs.com/collections/eq-i-2-0.
17 Gallup, "State of the American Workplace," published February
    6, 2020. https://www.gallup.com/workplace/238085/state-
    american-workplace-report-2017.aspx?thank-you-report-form=1.

ABOUT THE AUTHOR

Nikki Pounds is a wife and mother first, and a Human Resources (HR) practitioner and entrepreneur second. She is an accomplished speaker and business executive with twenty-five years of HR and leadership development expertise and is the founder of HR Unequivocally® in Charlotte, North Carolina. She graduated from the University of South Carolina Spartanburg Campus with a Bachelor of Arts in Psychology and earned a Master's degree in Human Resource Development from Clemson University. Nikki holds both the Senior Professional in Human Resources (SPHR) and Society for Human Resource Management Certified Professional (SHRM-CP) certifications. HR Unequivocally® partners with organizations to create growth strategies involving all aspects of human capital management, leadership development, and diversity, equity, and inclusion. Nikki prides herself on ensuring that already powerful individuals feel empowered by offering the training, support, and guidance needed to meet and often exceed their goals.

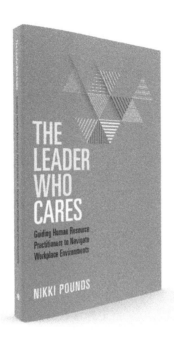

in linkedin.com/in/nikkipoundshr/

f @hrunequivocally

⊙ @hrunequivocally

🖥 https://hrugroup.com

✉ TheLeaderWhoCares@hrugroup.com